Kenny's Garage
by Kenny Wallace

Published by Waldorf Publishing
2140 Hall Johnson Road
#102-345
Grapevine, Texas 76051
www.WaldorfPublishing.com

Kenny's Garage
ISBN: 978-1-944784-52-2

Library of Congress Control Number: 2016935629

Copyright © 2016

All rights reserved. No part of this book may be reproduced or transmitted in any form or by any means whatsoever without express written permission from the author, except in the case of brief quotations embodied in critical articles and reviews. Please refer all pertinent questions to the publisher. All rights reserved. No part of this book may be reproduced or transmitted in any form or by any means, electronic or mechanical, including photocopying, recording, or by an information storage and retrieval system except by a reviewer who may quote brief passages in a review to be printed in a magazine or newspaper without permission in writing from the publisher.

Book Dedication

I would like to dedicate this book to my wife and my three daughters who have throughout the years depended on me to take care of their cars. This book "Kenny's Garage" is a great book. It is an extension to your cars owner's manual to teach you how to check your tire pressure, check and change your oil, check and replenish your fluids, how to buy and sell a car, prepare for a road trip, do simple to complex repairs and so much more.

I would also like to dedicate this book to my fans that have supported me throughout my career.

Special Thanks

To my momma Judy Wallace, when Rusty and Mike ran off to the racetrack, my mom took time to take care of me when I was not old enough to get into the pit gate. She also put me on her lap and taught me how to drive on the back roads in Missouri. My mom is a tough lady; she lived with her parents in an apartment above a bar in Baltimore, Maryland and I love her.

Special Mentions

I would like to thank my sponsors and partners with whom I have great relationships. I really care about them, and I am proud of them.

Toyota: They are a great group of people that I really enjoy. I have a lot of fun working with them. They are first class. I have been to Blue Springs, Mississippi to their Toyota Corolla plant and I have watched Corolla's being built. Toyota employs a quarter of a million Americans directly and indirectly. They are very innovative and leave no stone unturned as they are always striving to be better. In auto racing they give me all of the tools that I need to compete. I am proud that I am the first modified dirt race car in the United States to run a V8 Toyota motor. It has been fun to develop, and it has a lot of horsepower. We win with this motor!

JEGS: I appreciate my relationship with them and admire their awesome family. They have kept up with modern times and are good to their word while running a solid business.

American Ethanol: It is a high performance fuel and this is why Henry Ford started using it in 1890. There has been 10% ethanol in all gas pumps since the 1970's. A lot of people are threatened by ethanol. We are trying to cut down on our dependency on foreign oil, so by using ethanol, it keeps jobs here in the United States and allows farmers to make money.
I want to give a huge shout out to our farmers, without them we would be up a creek without a canoe or paddle!

University of Northwestern Ohio: They are the rarest of all colleges in the world. You can go to college there and get a business degree, you can play sports and they are a premier motorsports college. You can literally go there and learn how to work on race cars. They teach you how to build motors. They teach you how to weld, how to set-up race cars, then you can join their racing team as they race every weekend at Limaland Speedway. It is an incredible college.

FOX Sports 1: It has been a lot of fun working with them. They recognize me as the NASCAR driver that has 900 NASCAR starts. They know my background, respect me, and allow me a lot of leeway to give my opinion.

They value my experience and let me use my experience of running the Daytona 500, running the Southern 500, the Brickyard 400 and my road course experience. They allow me to tell the fans what I think every weekend without editing me. I have so much fun working with FOX Sports 1!
Kenny Wallace

Book Foreword by Kenny Schrader

I am thrilled and honored to write the forward for this book, and thrilled that Kenny would ask me. I like doing anything for Kenny.

This book is a great fit for Kenny Wallace to release. He knows so much about buying and selling cars, preparing your car and yourself for a road trip or seasonal travel, and how to work and maintain a car. He also has lots of tips to give car owners that will save a lot of aggravation with mechanical issues or buying the wrong car.

I am nine years older than Kenny. When I first met him, he was just a little guy. He has always had 'out of control' enthusiasm, and he will wear you out in a heartbeat, but not wear himself out. I taught Kenny how to drive sitting in my lap in a 14-acre field, and we did not hit anything too hard! No matter what project he puts himself into, he hits it hard.

A funny story that I remember about Kenny is when his brothers were heading to a race in their hauler. They stopped for gas at a truck stop, but did not know that Kenny had crawled out of the back! They were an hour away before they realized that they had left him there! Keep in mind that this was way before cell phones, so there was no way to reach Rusty and Mike to let them know Kenny had been left behind. Finally, about an hour down the road, the highway patrol stopped Rusty and Mike, and asked them if they were missing anybody. Kenny was about thirteen years old and was a bit devastated when he discovered Rusty and Mike were gone!

Kenny is so committed to racing, and he has been able to make it work. It is very tough to make a living at racing and to do full-time, but Kenny has been able to make it all work. He has had a very successful racing career in NASCAR's Nationwide and Sprint Cup Series, and with his personality and enthusiasm he really shines on TV. People want to think of Kenny as a TV guy, but he is a racer, first and foremost. Kenny has a natural ability to entertain on TV, so he is following that career as well.

Kenny's Dad was a really good dirt racer, and his brother Mike is also a really good dirt racer. Kenny helped Mike a lot with his dirt racing, and he was always around the dirt tracks. But he went pavement racing and never really got to run dirt. Once Kenny ran dirt a couple of times, he fell in love with it. He has a very nice operation and team. I helped him get started in dirt racing, and he is very good at it. He has always enjoyed it and is very serious about it.

I like racing against Kenny on dirt, it is a blast. No matter what happens in that race, Kenny always make sure that we are going to have a good time afterwards by talking to the fans, having a drink and jacking around with each other.

Kenny Wallace is like a combination of a younger brother and best friend. He means a lot to me, he is a very dear friend and a buddy of mine.

Kenny Schrader

Table of Contents

Your Car is not a UFO 1
Back to the Basics 4
Car Fluids 4
Checking Engine Oil 4
Checking Power Steering Fluid 6
Checking Automatic Transmission Fluid 7
Checking the Radiator Coolant 8
Checking the Clutch and Brake Fluid 9
Checking Battery Electrolyte 11
Checking Windshield Wiper Fluid 12

Open Heart Surgery 14
Dealing with Your Car's Innards and Limbs 14
Fuel Tank and Fuel Line 15
Exhaust 15
Driveline 15
Springs 15
Struts/Shock Absorbers 15
Brakes 15

Battery and Battery Posts 17

Heating and Cooling 20
Radiator and Heating Hoses 20
Air Cleaner Element 20
Spark Plugs and Wires 21
Fan Belt and Drive Belts 22
The Almighty Tune Up 22

Proper Maintenance of Your Metal Driving Machine — 23
Fluid Levels — 23
Fluid Replacement — 24
Rust Prevention — 24
Service Appointments — 24
Lighting and Electrical Systems — 25
Lights — 25

Tires and Wheels: Your Life is Riding on it — 27
Checking Tire Pressure — 27
How to Change a Tire — 29
Tire Safety — 29
Jacking Up Your Car and Removing the Lug Nuts — 30
Replace the Flat Tire with the Spare — 31
Ready to Roll to the Tire Store — 31
Tire Tread — 31
Wheel Balance — 32
Wheel Alignment — 33
Final Tire Advice and Tips — 33

Getting the Most Out of Your Buck at the Gas Pump — 35

Driving Tips that Save Time and Money — 38
Check Your Fluids Before you Drive — 39
Measure the Tread on Your Tires — 39
Check Your Windshield Wiper Blades — 39
Brakes — 40
Pack Emergency Provisions — 40
GPS — 40

Safety Tips	40
Preparing You and Your Car for a Road Trip	43
Car Emergency Kit	45
Tips for Winter Weather Driving and Maintaining Your Car in Winter Weather	48
Prepping Your Car For Summer	54
What to do after an Accident	56
How to Get the Most Value When Selling Your Car	58
Preparing to Sell Your Car	58
Dents and Dings	59
Filling-in Small Scratches	61
Keeping Your Cars Resale Value	62
Applying a Carpet and Upholstery Protector to Your Car's Interior	63
Applying a Clear Coat Protector to Your Car's Paint	64
Things to Keep in Mind when Buying a Car	65
Car Buying Advice	66
Options That May or May Not Suit Your Needs	69
All-Wheel Drive	69
4-Door Vehicle	70
Gas Mileage	70
Color Selection	70
Extended Warranty	71
Used Vehicle Mechanical Inspection	71

Understanding that Sticky Sticker Price	71
Used Car Shopping	73
Looking for Possible Paintwork	75
What about Car Insurance	76
How-To Segments	78
How to Change Your Oil Change	79
How to Switch Out Your Spark Plugs	80
How to Change Your Air Filter	81
How to Check Belts	82
How to Switch Out Your Distributor Cap	83
How to Talk Kenny Schrader into Teaching you How to Drive Dirt Car	84
How to Inspect and Adjust Misaligned Headlights	86
How to Replace a Headlamp	87
How to Replace a Brake Light Bulb	88
How to Replace a Turn Signal Bulb	89
How to Replace a Headlight Switch	90
How to Replace a Blown Fuse	91
How to Replace a Starter	93
How to Replace a Water Pump	94
How to Replace an Alternator	96
How to Replace the Alternator Belt	98
How to Replace a Fog Light Assembly	100
How to Jumpstart a Car	101
How to Install a Battery	103
How to Replace Door Weather Stripping	105
How to Replace a Window Regulator	106
How to Replace the Cabin Air Filter	108
How to Inspect the A/C Compressor	108
How to Inspect the A/C Condenser	109

How to Inspect the A/C Line or Hose	109
How to Inspect the A/C System	110
How to Inspect the A/C Heater Blower	111
How to Replace the A/C Heater Blower	112
How to Replace the Heater Core Hoses	113
How to Replace the Upper Radiator Hose	114
How to Replace the Transmission Cooler Lines	115
How to Check Brake Fluid Level	116
How to Perform a Brake Adjustment	117
How to Replace a Brake Booster	118
How to Replace the Brake Calipers	119
How to Replace a Brake Drum	121
How to Flush Brake Fluid	122
How to Perform a Front Disc Brake Job	123
How to Replace a Master Cylinder	125
How to Replace Brake Pads	126
How to Replace a Brake Pedal Switch	127
How to Replace a Brake Disc (or Rotor)	128
How to Perform a Brake Safety Inspection	129
How to Replace the Brake Shoes	130
How to Bleed Brakes with a Tool and with a Helper	132
How to Check Power Steering Fluid Level	133
How to Replace a Power Steering Pump	133
How to Replace the Power Steering Rack	135
How to Replace Coil Springs	136
How to Replace a Ball Joint	137
How to Replace the Air Intake Boot	138
How to Replace a Serpentine Belt	139
How to Replace a V-Belt	141
How to Replace an Ignition Coil	141
How to Replace an Engine Freeze Plug	143

How to Clean Your Fuel System	144
How to Replace a Catalytic Converter	144
How to Replace a Wiper Blade	145
How to Replace a Wiper Motor	146
How to Replace a Wiper Switch	148
Some Easy Odds and Ends	150
How to Adjust a Hood Release Latch	150
How to Replace a Hood Emblem	150
How to Replace a Window Belt Strip	151
How to Troubleshoot a Check Engine Light	152
Closing Thoughts	154
Kenny Wallace Bio	155
Credits	157

Kenny's Garage   Kenny Wallace

Your Car is Not a UFO

Yes, a UFO, as in an unidentified flying object. Cars are not impossible to work on when the mystery is taken out of the "unidentified objects" under the hood. The mechanisms used in the first automobiles are similar to the complex, computerized mechanisms of today. Our cars still run on oil, transmission fluid, power steering fluid, brake fluid, anti-freeze, and still cushion the road with a set of four tires.

I meet so many people who do not know what the air pressure should be in their tires. I meet people who have no control over their car. If it is low on oil, they spend too much money to get the oil checked and changed. Besides a home, a car is the second largest investment that we make. Our cars are what get us from point A to point B, and it is such an important piece in our lives that we just cannot afford to have any problems with it. There are so many things that we need to know about our cars and this book will walk you through that needed information.

I put this book together because I would like to offer consumers an extension of their owner's manual. It picks-up where your owner's manual leaves off.

Keep this book handy. It offers; a how-to book with buying and selling tips, easy maintenance and mechanical instruction, road trip preparation and so much more. It's basically a bumper-to-bumper guide with a plethora of information about your car and funny stories blended in for a chuckle!

I have compiled my lifelong history with cars, trucks, tractors; you name it in order to write this book. However, I will warn you, working on your car and feeling empowered can be very addicting.

Learning to change your oil for the first time is as easy as baiting a hook or making Macaroni and Cheese from a box!

You must always think and remember safety first!
You can never be too careful when working on your car. Always make certain that the car is parked on a level surface, the emergency brake is engaged, the engine has been turned off, cooled off and consider wearing gloves and goggles.

By doing your own repairs you will be able to keep more money in your pocket by not having to always depend on a mechanic. By doing your own regular scheduled maintenance, you will save hundreds or thousands of dollars on future repairs by keeping your car as healthy as possible.

Kenny's Garage   Kenny Wallace

I will also say this, when in doubt refer to your car's manufacturer or local trusted mechanic. I am offering a ton of advice in this book, but not all of my advice will fit every make and model out there.

Back to the Basics

Car Fluids
I realize that the majority of our population would say that there is nothing basic or simple about the innards of a vehicle. However, I promise that once you have a little knowledge, your automobile is not going to appear as complex as you think.

Let's take a look under the hood of your car. One of the most basic aspects of your car is learning how to maintain proper fluid levels. This is a necessity to keeping your car's health in good order.

In order to insure your safety, always make sure that your car has been turned off for at least an hour before you start messing around under the hood so that you do not burn yourself. Although these fluids represent a variety of uses within your car, checking each one of them is very similar.

Checking Engine Oil
Checking the level of oil in the engine is one of the most important and easiest maintenance tasks that you can perform on your vehicle.

Park your vehicle on a level surface. Turn the engine off and engage the emergency brake. Allow the engine to cool, then prop the hood open securely. You may choose to wear gloves and goggles as an extra precaution.

Check your owner's manual for the location of the dipstick. Usually the dipstick is located on the front side of the engine, and most dipsticks have a yellow handle.

Remove the dipstick and use a clean rag or paper towel to wipe off the excess oil. The oil should be a golden honey color.

When you look at the end of the dipstick you will find two marks that show the lowest and highest recommended levels. Put the dipstick back in, then pull it out. Look to see where the oil level comes to. You will want the oil level to be near the top of the crosshatches…the little railroad track looking design midway up the stick. Repeat the procedure to help ensure that you get an accurate reading.

If you find that you are low on oil, determine what grade of oil you should add to your car by referring to your owner's manual or by determining what type the automotive technician used the last time you had an oil change. Keep in mind that as your car gets older and accumulates more miles, you will want to consider switching to a different grade of oil.

Once you have determined the proper grade, add a half a quart of oil at a time, using a plastic funnel to avoid spillage. Check between each addition to see when the oil is at the proper level. You don't want to overfill the tank unless you're just in the mood to buy a new engine.

Remember to get your oil changed every 3,000 miles unless you are running on synthetic. Or if you seem to be topping off your oil frequently, have your vehicle checked by your local trusted mechanic.

While you are driving, routinely check your oil gauge or oil warning light. Do not run your engine if no oil is showing on the dipstick or if your oil gauge or warning light is indicating a low oil pressure or level.

If you spilled a little oil on your engine when you were filling your oil, you may notice a burning odor when you drive your vehicle. This should only last for a short period of time as the oil burns off. If you have any unusual smells coming from your vehicle, take it to your local trusted mechanic immediately for a further inspection.

Checking Power Steering Fluid
A friend of mine once thought her teenage son had the common sense to pour power steering fluid in her husband's truck. Handing the bottle of fluid to the eager son she asked "Are you SURE you know where it goes?" A few rolled eyes and "Oh Mom's" later, she was on her way. About two weeks later, the brakes locked up and there was

smoke everywhere. "What in the world???" Somebody put power steering fluid in the brake fluid reservoir!

The power steering reservoir is under the hood. It's easy to check the level and top it off if necessary.

It's a simple matter of checking the dipstick (no, not your husband or your wife), much like the one for the engine oil, but usually the fluid is added through the filter neck of the reservoir. Many vehicles have clear windows with level indicators. You can see the level at a glance.

On some vehicles, you check the level with the engine running, and on others, the engine must be off. Refer to your owner's manual for your vehicle.

Before topping off, stop the engine to prevent any danger of coming into contact with moving parts.
Power steering fluid should be checked, especially if you hear the power steering whining when making turns. You also may need a new power steering pump if the whining persists.

Checking Automatic Transmission Fluid
Once again, it is a matter of checking a dipstick. Since all vehicles are different, you will need to check your owner's manual to find the location of the dipstick and the grade of fluid required. Most transmission dipsticks are located

toward the back of the engine.

Most manufacturers specify that the fluid level be checked with the automatic transmission at operating temperature. This can sometimes require a drive of up to two miles, or you may simply check it after running a few errands.

Make sure the vehicle is parked on level ground and the emergency brake is engaged.

Usually the level is checked with the engine idling and the transmission in "park." Use a funnel to replenish the fluid if it is low, adding half a quart at a time and checking between each addition as you would with your oil. Transmission fluid should have a rich, red color.

Take your vehicle to a manufacturer or mechanic for further inspection if you notice any of the following: if the level is down excessively, if the reservoir requires frequent topping off, if the fluid has a dark color or a burnt smell, or if you can see metal type flakes on the dipstick.

Checking Radiator Coolant
The vehicle's cooling system can be very dangerous. Coolant in the radiator at normal operating temperature is near its boiling point and under extreme pressure, so be very careful.

Kenny's Garage   Kenny Wallace

Check the coolant levels weekly, and make sure that the system has cooled down before touching anything to avoid serious burns.

To remove the radiator cap, press down as you undo the cap. The radiator must be filled to the top.

If it needs to be topped off, use only the correct coolant, as specified in your owner's manual. Adding the right mixture to your coolant system is important, especially in the winter. You should have a mixture of half antifreeze and half water. You can check the level by looking at the overflow. The coolant fluid should be a nice lime green color.

Some vehicles have an overflow or reservoir system with a clear plastic reservoir. The fluid level should be between the two marks on the side. With this system, you only need to remove the reservoir cap to check the level each month.

Don't drive a vehicle with a cooling system leak or other problem. If the engine in your vehicle has overheated, both the engine and the cooling system will need to be tested by your local mechanic.

Checking Clutch and Brake Fluid
Vehicles with manual transmissions have either a cable operated clutch or a hydraulically operated clutch.

If your vehicle has a hydraulically operated clutch, you will have to check the fluid in the master cylinder. You should also check the brake master cylinder at the same time.

The clutch and brake master cylinders are usually located on the rear wall of the engine bay. The same type of brake fluid is used in both. Refer to your owner's manual for the specifications. Using the wrong fluid or other fluids, such as engine oil or water, can cause clutch or brake failure.

Most vehicles have "see-through" plastic reservoirs with level marks, so you can clearly see if the fluid is at the correct level. Some vehicles share the same reservoir for clutch and brake fluid.

When the fluid level drops slightly, it needs to be topped off.

Before removing the reservoir cap, clean around the area. Dirt, water and other materials will contaminate the fluid, which can affect the clutch and/or brake systems.
Use a funnel to add fluid.

It is recommended that you don't remove the cap unless absolutely necessary. Keep the reservoir and cap clean and replace the cap as soon as you finish. It is also recommended that you only use newly opened brake fluid.

Kenny's Garage   Kenny Wallace

Brake fluid can damage your paint. When topping off reservoirs, be extremely careful not to spill or splash it. Keep a rag handy to immediately mop up any spills, and wash off the paint with water.

If fluid levels are excessively or consistently low, take your vehicle to a mechanic for further inspection.

Checking Battery Electrolyte
Some batteries require water and some do not. Again, before working on your car, make sure that the motor has been turned off so that it is cool before you start tinkering around under the hood. Adding water to the battery is as simple as popping off the cover or covers on top of the battery and topping it off.

The correct electrolyte level in the battery is essential for efficient operation and should be checked regularly. The electrolyte needs to completely cover the active plates in the battery.

You can see the level either through the side of the case (if it is a clear plastic type) or by unscrewing or popping the caps to each cell. Some modern batteries, however, need no maintenance at all, so they are completely sealed.

Use distilled water. Normal tap water can contain damaging minerals, which will shorten the battery's life.

The electrolyte is an acid, which can damage skin, clothes or your vehicle's paint. Clean up any spills with plenty of water and make sure the battery top is clean and dry. Make sure that you wash your hands afterwards.

If your vehicle does not start easily, or your battery or generator indicator light comes on, or if you notice any corrosion on the battery terminals, take your vehicle to your local mechanic.

Windshield Wiper Fluid
We are spoiled now, a push of a button and your windshield can be sparkling clean! Not so years ago, my friend told me a story of her trip to Yellowstone National Park in 1960. With so few stores and rest stops along the road, you always had to be prepared. Of course food, drinks and his Dad's "6 pack of beer" were a must. "What is that ahead? Could it be a dust storm? No a 'bug storm'!" Thousands of juicy bugs hit the windshield! Of course they turned the windshield wipers on to make matters worse.

"What to do? Can't see out of this…hmmm…kids, hand me your Kool-Aid!" Heck no, you could not pry it out of their hands. As a last resort the prized "6 pack" looked like a good substitute for window cleaner. Six empty cans later and a few dead bugs we were on our way. Only problem was our car smelled like it had taken a beer bath when we arrived!

Kenny's Garage   Kenny Wallace

I realize this isn't under the hood, but since we have been talking about fluids, it felt appropriate to talk about now. These days, windshield wiper fluid is usually in see-through plastic reservoirs. Use a funnel to fill up your reservoir with windshield washer fluid.

Ordinary washing detergent is not suitable. Detergent plays havoc on your wiper blades, washer nozzles and paint. Ordinary household detergents can leave streaks.

The jet of water from the washers should hit the windshield in the center of each wiper's sweep.

If the flow is not as good as it used to be, the washer jets can be cleared using a fine needle or pin. Don't use force, or the jets may become misaligned or damaged.

Most washer jets can also be re-aimed using the same needle.

Oil from exhaust fumes, road grime and dead bugs build up on the windshield, so a regular wipe with a good quality glass cleaner will help improve visibility and help extend the life of the wiper.

Open Heart Surgery
Dealing with Your Car's Innards and Limbs

I realize that when most people open the hood of their car and look inside it feels like they are looking at something as complex as heart or brain surgery. Trust me; cars are simple, basic machines. Let me introduce you to what's under your car's hood.

Funny story first:
My dear friend Kenny Schrader is a race car driver, but he use to work for an oil company out of St. Louis, Missouri. He needed to make money during the winter time, because he raced the rest of the time. So the oil company told him, "We need you to take the gas truck out to this big construction site and fill up the earth movers out there with fuel." So Schrader took that big gas truck out to the construction site to fill up the earth movers with diesel fuel, and mistook the hydraulic oil for where the gas was supposed to go. He filled the hydraulic oil container with gas. Schrader then called the oil company and told them, "Man this truck only took a couple of gallons of gas." They said, "Kenny, where was the cap that you put gas into?" So Kenny said, "Right by the driver's door." The oil company said, "Kenny, that was the hydraulic oil cap, where the hydraulic oil is to go!"

Fuel Tank and Fuel Line
The fuel tank holds the fuel while the line takes it to the engine.

Exhaust
After the engine burns the fuel-air mixture, the emissions are taken out of the vehicle through the exhaust system.

Driveline
The differential has a couple of functions, including transmitting power to the wheels while allowing them to rotate at different speeds when turning or traveling on slippery surfaces.

Springs
Coil or leaf springs carry the weight of the vehicle and absorb the bumps.

Struts/Shock Absorbers
The struts/shock absorbers are found near each wheel and control the amount of vehicle movement when it goes over bumps.

Brakes
Good brakes are an essential part of safe motoring. They need to be checked by your mechanic at least once a year. You should, however, become aware of the normal brake pedal travel and firmness. If you notice any change in the

application pressure, pedal height or feel, or hear a screeching sound, have the brakes inspected by your local mechanic immediately. Do not attempt to service your own brake system.

Let's walk through some simple and basic maintenance you can do to insure your car's longevity and save money in the long run.

Kenny's Garage   Kenny Wallace

Battery and Battery Posts

A famous "trick" is to carry a bottle of cola in your car to pour on your battery terminals to clean them. Yes it works, then you get to enjoy the rest!

Most batteries get dirty sitting in the engine bay. You will probably see a white ashy looking substance around one or both terminals. To keep a battery working well, make sure the terminals are clean and tight, and make sure the battery is securely mounted.

The battery contains poisonous and corrosive acid, and produces highly flammable and explosive hydrogen gas, so always use great care. In particular, avoid contact with skin and eyes. When working around a battery, always wear protective clothing and glasses. Do not smoke or light a match, and don't cause a spark.

To clean the terminals, you will need to disconnect the battery. Please note that on late model vehicles with computer management systems and electronic radios, the memory may be lost when you disconnect the battery; so make sure you have the radio security code before you disconnect it.

On all vehicles, care should be taken not to cause a short circuit with the tools. Disconnect the negative (–) lead first and reconnect it last. The battery is normally marked with (+), or red for positive, and (–), or black for negative.

There are two traditional methods to clean your battery posts, and one little trick of the trade that I will share with you.

1. You can use the old handy silver tool with the wire bristles inside of it. You simply slip the wire tool down onto the battery post and twist it around several times until the corrosion comes off.

2. You can buy a can of anti-corrosion spray and spray it directly onto the corroded post. Let it sit there for about 30 seconds and then wash away the excess with warm water. One of my brothers showed me this trick when I was little. Take a can of cola and pour some of it onto the corroded post. The carbonated cola will start bubbling up as it eats away the corrosion. Let it sit on there for about 30 seconds, and then wash it away with warm water! I have always been enamored with household tricks that you can use to do repairs or maintenance.

Make sure to clean your battery connectors as well. Then refit and tighten carefully.

After reconnecting the leads, smear some petroleum jelly on the terminals. This will help prevent buildup of deposits in the future. If the corrosion keeps appearing on the battery terminals, it indicates an electrolyte leak, and you should take the vehicle to your local mechanic.

By keeping the battery posts clean and clear of corrosion, you will increase the longevity of the life of your battery. I mean, who wants to have a dead battery when they are trying to be the first person to their favorite department store clearance sale?

Kenny's Garage   Kenny Wallace

Heating and Cooling

Yes, we are all spoiled when it comes to the atmosphere inside our home on wheels. You don't want surprises on a road trip to Las Vegas when your air might choose to go out! Do a little preventive maintenance before you leave the house.

Radiator and Heater Hoses

Every six months, with the engine cold, look over all the vehicle's hoses and squeeze them to check for any soft spots, hard spots, ballooning or any signs of cracking or splitting. If you have any doubts, go to your local mechanic.

Air Cleaner Element

Vehicle engines burn a mixture of fuel and oxygen. For efficient running, the air needs to be as clean as possible. This is the function of the air filter or air cleaner.

Every 12 months or every 12,000 miles, you can unscrew or unclip the air cleaner assembly and carefully lift out the old filter. If you drive your vehicle in dusty areas, it will need to be checked every 6 months or every 6,000 miles. Don't let any dirt or other trash fall into the air cleaner assembly. It leads into the engine and may cause severe engine damage.

Kenny's Garage   Kenny Wallace

Wipe out the inside of the air cleaner assembly. You may want to vacuum it out before putting everything back together.

It can be hard to determine whether an air cleaner element really needs replacing, but they are not expensive. It's probably wiser to simply replace it if you are unsure. Ensure the new filter is correctly located, and the air cleaner assembly is properly fitted and secured.

Spark Plugs and Wires
Spark plugs are a wearing part. As their condition deteriorates, the engine does not run as smoothly. Performance is reduced and fuel consumption increases. Exhaust emission output will also increase.

With the introduction of more efficient electronic engine management systems and platinum-tipped spark plugs, the service and replacement interval on some vehicles has increased dramatically. Refer to your owner's manual for the correct type of spark plugs and recommended replacement intervals.

Carefully check the plug wires and plug connections in case they're cracked, damaged or not fitted correctly. If it looks like they need replacing or refitting, or the vehicle is running roughly, visit a mechanic.

Fan Belt and Drive Belts

One word of caution: If you have cats, always look under the hood in the winter. They love to crawl under the hood and stay warm. No need for fur to fly when you crank your engine!

A broken belt can result in costly engine damage and travel delays.

Belts deteriorate with age and operation. They need to be checked regularly, adjusted and occasionally replaced.

The belt should be closely inspected for fraying, cracking, excessive wear or oil contamination. If your fan belt looks worn, have it replaced immediately.

Pay particular attention to replacement intervals if your vehicle is fitted with a rubber cam or timing belt. Failure to replace will cause serious engine damage. Replacement intervals are determined by miles or time, whichever comes first. If it's time for a replacement, your mechanic can help.

The Almighty Tune-Up

I cringe at the thought of a tune-up. It's just one more expense for my car that I really don't want. Yet, tune-ups are important. Compare them to a yearly physical; you want to make sure everything is in proper working order. You can perform a basic tune-up at home.

Kenny's Garage   Kenny Wallace

Proper Maintenance of Your Metal Driving Machine

The biggest issue we face as car owners is proper vehicle maintenance. Our cars are a huge investment. We want to protect that investment; not only for performance reasons, but also for resale value, should we decide to sell the car in the future.

I have a rule around my house with my daughters. When they turn 25 years old, they become responsible for their bills. Hopefully at this time they will also become responsible for their cars!

We need to think of our car's health like our body's health: run the right fluids through both and get regularly scheduled checkups.

Working around your car is pretty simple if you learn the basics like checking and maintaining the fluids, checking the air in your tires, changing a tire before it blows out, the proper way to detail your car, etc.

Here are a few tips to quickly educate you on basic maintenance:

Fluid Levels
I cannot stress how important it is to maintain proper fluid levels underneath the hood (or trunk if you drive a

Porsche). Checking and maintaining fluids (i.e. oil, transmission fluid, washer fluid, and brake fluid) is as simple as downloading a song off of the Internet. I understand many people fear getting under the hood of their car, but once you've learned the process, you can almost do it in your sleep.

Fluid Replacement
It is not enough to just keep the correct level of the fluids described above. You must also replace the fluids frequently to keep them clean. Dirty oil is almost as bad as low oil. Oil is the lifeblood of our vehicle. Think of it like water for our bodies.

Rust Prevention
To help reduce the potential of a rust problem, particularly if you live in a snowy climate, I recommend washing your vehicle at least once a week during the winter.

Additionally, to help prevent your car from being attacked by rust, have the car's undercarriage coated with a rust protector.

Service Appointments
Make sure you bring your car in for the recommended service appointments covered by your warranty. Also, pay attention to warning messages/lights sent by your vehicle's monitoring system.

Lighting and Electrical Systems

Us Wallace's always try to abide by the rules. We had a taillight that got smashed somehow in a vehicle we use to drive when I was about 10 years old. I remember Rusty taking a flashlight, turning it on and putting a red shop towel around it which made the light red and then we taped it in the broken out area. This is what we did. We had no money. We were under middle class. It started out that this was going to be a very temporary fix, but as time went on and as it got dark outside, it was just too easy to turn on that flashlight wrapped in a red shop towel.

Lights

Properly functioning headlights, brake lights and indicator lights are essential for the safety of yourself, your family and others. They provide you with better vision, allow others to see you, and show others your intentions. Light bulbs can burn out at any time, so regular checks are important.

The easiest way to check lights is with two people, one to work the lights, one to check them.

If you can't find a helper, you can do it on your own by switching each light on and walking around the vehicle. To check the brake lights, position the vehicle so you can see the lights' reflection on a wall, the garage door or shop window.

There are a number of different types of bulbs and fittings used in a vehicle. The most common is the bayonet type, which is changed by pushing and twisting, similar to a household bulb. Most modern vehicles will indicate on the dash if a light is faulty. If your vehicle's lights are not functioning properly, visit a mechanic.

Kenny's Garage   Kenny Wallace

Tires and Wheels: Your Life is Riding on it

Your tires are as important as your shoes! Can't run a marathon in High Heels, Flip-Flops or Cleats.

Checking Tire Pressure

Today there are too many gadgets available to check the air in your tires. I prefer to use to the $2.00 special that looks like a pen, which can be picked up at most convenience stores. You can also buy digital tire gauges these days that will give you a digital illuminated reading on the display screen.

To determine the proper air pressure your tires require, you will need to refer to the door jam on the driver's door of the vehicle or to your owner's manual.

Note: This is true if the tires that are on the car are the same size as when they came from the factory. If the tires are a different size than the original ones, you will need to refer to the make, model and tire size you have now. Most tire stores can offer assistance to determine the proper and correct tire air pressure that is required for your tires.

The procedure is fairly simple. Unscrew the tire stem cover and place the tire gauge onto the tire stem. Press down and hold it firmly until you have the reading. Read the gauge and determine how much air is needed, if any. If you are in need of air, add air, and then re-check until you reach the proper air pressure required in your tires. Repeat this process for each tire. Always remember to replace the tire stem cover as air can leak out.

I would recommend checking the tire pressure when the tires are not too cold or too hot. Check them after you run a couple of errands.

While checking the air in your tires, make sure to check all four tires and check the condition of your spare tire as well. You do not want to be out driving only to find that you have a flat spare when you need it. That would definitely mean incurring an unnecessary roadside repair expense, or taking a long, long walk.

You can check the air pressure in all four tires in the amount of time it would take you to fill your car up with gasoline.

To get the most life out of your tires and the smoothest ride possible, have your tires rotated and high-speed balanced every 5,000 miles. Remember that most tires have a life of anywhere from 40,000 to ,60,000 miles, so replace tires on a timely basis to insure a safe ride for you, your family, and other drivers on the road.

Kenny's Garage					Kenny Wallace

Remember that tires are the only things that cushion your car to the road. So for safety, please take your tires seriously.

How to Change a Tire
Working around your car can be as fun as winning a prestigious award. Most people tend to think of their car as some sort of foreign object that will explode if they touch it. Changing a tire is like learning how to ride a bicycle; once you do it you will never forget how. This skill will also enable you to change your own tire instead of waiting for help, which can typically take a few hours. Plus, it will allow you to keep more money in your pocket by not having to pay someone to change the tire for you.

Tire Safety
Always remember to put safety first whenever working on and around your car.

Park your car on a flat surface, and engage the emergency brake. Make sure to turn off the car, and remove the keys from the ignition. If you break down and end up on the side of a road or freeway, make sure to use road safety devices on all four corners of your vehicle to alert oncoming traffic that you have had a breakdown. There are thousands of deaths every year caused by people who do not use proper road safety devices such as flares or reflective triangles. It is better to be over prepared then underprepared, so I suggest putting wheel blocks or chucks on both sides of the three tires that you will not be working on.

You may choose to wear gloves and safety glasses when changing your tire.

Jacking up your Car and Removing the Lug Nuts
Get the car jack and the tire iron out of the trunk or rear of your vehicle and loosen all of the lugs from the wheel before jacking your car up. When loosening the lug nuts, you may have to use a little force or elbow grease (that's effort down South)! You just want to loosen them. Do not totally remove them at this point.

Position the jack on the ground directly under a part of your car's frame. Refer to your owner's manual for the exact positioning of the jack.

Most car jacks these days are a screw-type scissor jack, which means you simply turn the knob at the end of the jack using the provided metal hand crank. Raise the jack until it makes contact with the car's frame and continue raising the car with the jack until the flat tire is completely raised off the ground.

You can now remove the lug nuts and place them in a safe place so that you can locate them when putting on the spare tire.

Kenny's Garage   Kenny Wallace

It is also a good idea to place the flat tire under the car for extra safety precaution in case something fails with the jack.

Replace the Flat Tire with the Spare
Now it is time to position the spare tire over your wheel studs and replace the lug nuts. I suggest using your foot as a balancing device while putting the lug nuts back onto the wheel. First, use your own strength to tighten the lug nuts to make sure that you have them aligned onto the studs correctly until they feel snug. Now get the tire iron and use as much torque as you can muster to tighten them down.

Carefully lower the jack to let your car down until it is flush with the ground and check to see if it is possible to tighten the lugs anymore at this point.

Ready to Roll to the Tire Store
Put the flat tire in the back of your vehicle and find your way to a local tire store. If you drive a compact car and your spare is a doughnut tire, then remember that doughnut tires are designed to drive a maximum of 50 miles distance at 50 MPH.

Tire Tread
While checking tire pressure, also look for tire wear or damage.

Obviously, you shouldn't let the treads wear too low. All tires have built-in indicators to show when they are worn too far.

As a general rule, if the tread is not as deep as the head of a match, it is unsafe and illegal. You can also check the wear by putting a penny upside down into the tread. If you can see any of Lincoln's head, you should invest in new tires.

If there is noticeably uneven wear, the wheel may need re-balancing, or there maybe something wrong with the steering alignment. Either way, your local mechanic can advise you of the correct course of action.

Your mechanic will also check for any damage to the tire wall, such as splits or cracking.

Wheel Balance
A vibration in the steering wheel or your seat while driving may indicate that the wheels are out of balance. This can be caused by hitting a stationary object with your wheels, such as bumping into the curb while parking. Wheel balancing will correct this situation.

Shaking in the steering wheel while braking is normally associated with your brakes. Your local mechanic can advise you on the correct course of action.

Kenny's Garage   Kenny Wallace

Wheel Alignment

One method of checking wheel alignment is to see if there is any "pulling" of the vehicle's steering. While driving, momentarily let go of your steering wheel. If your vehicle veers to the left or right, this is an indication that you may require a wheel alignment. Be very careful not to lose control of your vehicle.

Another method is to check the inside and outside edges of your tire for uneven or fast wear.

Wheel alignments cannot be performed at home. Make sure to visit your local mechanic.

Final Tire Advice and Tips

If you check the condition of your tires and keep the proper air pressure in them on a regular basis, you will reduce the risk of a flat tire. Also, check the condition of your spare tire every couple of months to make sure it is healthy enough to use if you are unfortunate enough to experience a flat tire.

You will also want to have your tires rotated and high-speed balanced every six months. This will assure even wear on your tires and allow for the safest and smoothest ride possible. It will also maximize the longevity of your tires.

Kenny's Garage   Kenny Wallace

Check the air pressure in your tires about once a month. This can be done in the same amount of time that it takes to fill up your car with gas.

To determine the proper air pressure for your tires, refer to the driver's side door jam or your owner's manual. You can also get the make, model and size of your tire from the tire's sidewall and call a local tire store for the proper PSI (pounds per square inch).

Kenny's Garage   Kenny Wallace

Getting the Most Out of Your Buck at the Gas Pump

This is a really funny story… while it was happening anyway…I decided to get a 300-gallon gas tank and put it in my shop due to the fact that we were always filling up lawnmowers, four-wheelers and quite a few cars. This would keep us from running up charges on our credit cards. I had Propst Brothers come out and fill up my 300-gallon gas tank every two weeks. This 300-gallon gas tank was also intended to fill up my car, my wife's cars, my daughters' cars and random lawnmowers, etc. However, one morning, I looked out the window and saw my daughter pushing her car up to that 300-gallon gas tank.

She ran out of gas the day before and did not want to stop at the gas station and spend her own money, but she was lucky enough to coast her car out of gas car into the driveway. My daughters were totally loving this gas tank and running their cars completely out of gas and then filling them up. When I was out of town at a race, they would drive my car until they ran it out of gas and then my wife's car until it was out of gas! Every time Kim and I would get home from a race weekend, I would have to say "time out!" Okay, now let's talk about the ever-rising cost of gasoline which takes the enjoyment out of going for those long, relaxing Sunday drives. Our wallets always seem to be getting lighter because of draining gas costs, so follow these tips to maximize your gas mileage and to keep more money where it belongs, in your pocket!

Tip 1: Having the proper air pressure in your tires actually burns less gas, and a decent bit, so check your air pressure about once a month. Remember to check your air pressure when the tires are cold.

Tip 2: Having regularly scheduled oil changes and filter replacements will also get you better gas mileage. Refer to the manufacturer to see what is recommended for your car.

Tip 3: Driving too fast and accelerating too quickly wastes fuel. Fast starts and hard breaking also wastes fuel, plus it is extremely hard on your engine.

Tip 4: Having roof racks and extra cargo increases the weight and wind resistance of your car. If you really don't need it, don't pack it, and remember to take heavy things out of your trunk instead of leaving them in there.

Tip 5: Another obvious thing is having a 4-cylinder engine instead of, let's say, an 8-cylinder engine. However, if you're like me, this is a moot point. I like the larger engines with more power regardless of gas guzzling.

Tip 6: Avoid excessive idling. If there is a long line at your favorite fast food drive-through, simply park and go in. You will also benefit the environment and your bank

Kenny's Garage   Kenny Wallace

account by burning less fuel and get a bit of exercise while walking to and from!

Oh, one more thing, switch out your air filter every 10,000-15,000 miles.

Driving Tips that Save Time and Money

It's always better to be over prepared than underprepared. Think of your car's health as you do your body's health. It's not going to last forever and is prone to breakdown if you don't take care of it. Isn't it better to be two steps ahead than to be broken down after venturing out on a trip?

I learned how to drive a car long before I should have, as most do. I was eight years old in a little town called Licking, Missouri. I was sitting in the lap of Kenny Schrader in his mom and dad's field in an old pick-up truck. He got in the truck, put me on his lap, and he let me steer. There was only one tree in the entire field and I ran into it. I will never forget this.

My mom "Judy" continued to teach me how to drive because my dad "Russ" was so busy. He was awesome. He worked so hard at King Dodge in downtown St. Louis, Missouri, and he also delivered newspapers. He was a hustler and a hardworking man, so he did not have a lot of time to teach me how to drive, as he was also busy raising a family.

Mom was a great driver too. She won Powder Puff races, and she won a lot of races in the St. Louis area at a little track called Lake Hill Speedway, in Valley Park, Missouri, and at Tri City Speedway in Granite City, Illinois. I love her so much. She was cool because she took me everywhere she went. There is a four-year difference between me and Mike, and seven years difference between me and Rusty, so they never wanted to take me anywhere.

Mom used to let me drive the back roads, and that is how I learned how to drive. She also took me to a cemetery, and I continued to learn how to drive in this cemetery in her lap. This was in Jefferson Barracks right outside St. Louis, Missouri.

Check your Fluids Before you Drive
Make sure you have proper levels of antifreeze, oil, transmission fluid, power steering fluid, brake fluid and windshield wiper fluid to ensure that everything is in top working order.

Measure the Tread on Your Tires
Correct tire tread and pressure is crucial for driving in rain and snow. You might consider investing in a set of snow tires for the winter.

Check your Windshield Wiper Blades
Change out windshield wiper blades at least twice a year or every 6,000 miles: spring for summer and fall for winter. Change your rear wiper blade at least once a year.

Brakes

Have you ever seen an action movie with a truck loaded with TNT rolling downhill but can't stop because the bad guys cut the brake fluid lines? Well, most likely that will never happen to you, but it could get pretty dramatic if you fail to keep your brakes in order.

Check your brakes and all of the braking components and get a tune-up for your car to keep your car in proper running order and help prevent a breakdown.

Pack Emergency Provisions

Water, snacks and items to keep you warm are good to have in case you break down in the middle of nowhere.

GPS

You may want to invest in a portable GPS System in order to help you navigate locally and on long road trips.
If you drive a truck, you may want to buy some bags of play sand (for sandboxes) and place them in the truck bed for extra traction on slick roads.

Safety Tips

I think we all have plenty of stories of doing things that we shouldn't have. My friend Steve Mahoney and I were partners in crime. His dad owned a company that had about 20 trucks, and so we took one of the trucks, popped it into neutral and rolled it down the hill until it started. We were driving it, and later on we stopped at a gas station. The gas station had a CB radio in it. We heard on the CB radio that there was an APB out for a stolen truck. Of course they were talking about us! We had not told his dad that we took the truck out for a joy ride!

Now let's talk a few safety tips:
1. Drive with your headlights on for safety.

2. Don't get overconfident with a four-wheel drive vehicle. It won't help you stop any faster.

3. Drivers should allow additional room between their vehicles and others.

4. Winter road conditions often result in longer stopping distances.

5. Avoid abrupt actions while steering, braking or accelerating, to lessen the chances of losing control of the vehicle.

6. Always be aware of other drivers on the road. Look farther ahead in traffic. Action by other drivers will alert you to problems and give you extra time to react. Stopping on snow and ice without skidding requires extra time and distance. If you have anti-lock brakes, press the pedal down firmly and hold it. If you don't have anti-lock brakes, gently pump the pedal. Either way, give yourself plenty of room to stop.

7. Avoid using cruise control or overdrive. Don't let your car make a bad decision for you.

Kenny's Garage   Kenny Wallace

Preparing You and Your Car for a Road Trip

My brothers Rusty and Mike, my Mom, Dad and I were heading to Daytona Beach Florida for Speed Week. It was a 16-17 hour road trip in my Dad's big yellow Ford/Lincoln Town Car. My Dad was so proud of it. We left St. Louis, and Rusty and Mike were fighting about sitting in the back seat. I was eight years old. I literally spent the entire time up in the rear window area where the stereo speakers were, in this big ole canary yellow Lincoln Town Car. Behind the back seat was that big shelf under the rear glass. I was the youngest and always got ruffed up, but I didn't care because I really wanted to go on this road trip. I always had the third child syndrome, so if Rusty or Mike tried to take advantage, I didn't care because I just wanted to go to Daytona. Plus, Rusty and Mike fought so bad that if I were to sit in the back seat with them, I would catch most of the punches they intended for each other! So I was happy to be sitting in the protected rear window area and rode the entire trip to Daytona just like that.

Millions of drivers take road trips every year. Who doesn't love a good road trip through the mountains, along the coast, or a nice drive with family and friends? The last thing you want to happen is a problem with your ride. Getting the car ready for a long drive is simple if you just take a few minutes to prepare.

First, let's discuss what mechanical issues you need to check out yourself or have a qualified mechanic check out before you go, and then we'll look at some of the essential items you need to have in your car before venturing out to your favorite destination.

Start by popping the hood and checking the main fluids that keep your car running. To properly check the oil, you will need to pull the dipstick out, wipe it off thoroughly and put it back in and pull it back out. When you pull it back out you will have your proper reading.

Next is the all-important transmission fluid if you drive an automatic. To check the transmission fluid, you will need to go through the same process as you did with the oil: pull out the transmission's dipstick, wipe it off, stick it back in and pull it back out. When you pull it back out you will have the proper reading.

Now let's check the radiator fluid. Your radiator should always maintain a half-antifreeze/half water mix. You can see the level of the fluid through your overflow container.

If you want to drive safely on the freeway and see clearly out of your windshield, make sure you have enough windshield wiper fluid in the car so you can clear all of those dead bugs and road grime. Make certain that your wiper blades are in good working condition.

Kenny's Garage   Kenny Wallace

Check to make certain that your belts and hoses are in good shape without any cracks or bubbled-up areas.

You should also have your tire pressure checked, but it is really easy to check yourself. Make sure to check all four tires and the air pressure and condition of your spare tire too.

Next, let's go over the items that you'll want to have in your car for safety and for essential use in case of emergencies.

Car Emergency Kit

Chocolate is optional but always good to have on hand. It is extremely important to have certain items in your car, just in case of a breakdown or an accident. You can never be too careful. These kits can be purchased at auto supply stores, or you can create your own.

First of all, acquire a container. I prefer a fishing tackle box because it has little compartments and shelves, and it's durable. These are the items I carry with me at all times, and if you want to add to this to customize your own emergency car kit, that's great!

Don't forget a gallon of water for a potential radiator issue or for being parched while stuck in hot weather. Make sure to pack a blanket in case you break down on the side of the road and it's freezing outside.

Kenny's Garage   Kenny Wallace

Here is the stuff you should always have handy just in case: a flashlight with extra batteries, road maps to guide you even if you have a GPS, because they don't show every road. Pack a box of Band-Aids, gauze and aspirin. Having non-perishable food is a good idea as well; protein bars, breakfast bars, dried fruit, trail mix, etc. Customize your kit with items that will suit you and the needs of your family members. If you have kids you may want to have extra games, DVD's and toys.

Safety road flares are important so you can signal other drivers in case of a breakdown. There were over 3,000 deaths on the road last year from cars breaking down without having the breakdown area safely secured.

A can of Tire Fix never hurts for a quick, temporary fix to that annoying flat tire.

Also have extra fluids on hand for a fill up or top off: a quart of oil, transmission fluid, brake fluid, power steering fluid, windshield wiper fluid, clutch fluid (if you are driving a standard transmission), and some antifreeze.

You'll always need jumper cables or a jump box, road trip or not, for a dead or weak battery. You never know when you may need to jump your car or someone else's. It is better to be over prepared than underprepared, and that

Kenny's Garage   Kenny Wallace

leads us to our next topic:

Tips for Winter Weather Driving and Maintaining Your Car in Winter Weather

1. Drive with your headlights on. Can't drive if you can't see!

2. Drive safely, according to weather conditions. Don't get overconfident with your four-wheel drive. It's all fun and games until you're upside down in a cornfield watching the snow trickle down on your totaled vehicle. Four-wheel drive won't help you stop any faster.

3. It is also important to wash your vehicle on a regular basis so you can get the salt off of the exterior. This will help prevent your car from rusting. If you can afford it, get the undercarriage sprayed with a preventive rust product.

4. Avoid using cruise control or overdrive. Don't let your car make a bad decision for you.

5. My suggestion for cutting down on snow glare would be to use your sun visor, wear a good pair of non-glare sunglasses, and keep your windshield as clean as possible inside and outside on a consistent basis.

6. Avoid abrupt actions while steering, braking or accelerating in an effort to lessen the chances of losing control of the vehicle. Look farther ahead in traffic. Action by other drivers will alert you to problems and will give you extra time to react.

7. Driving in torrential weather can be tricky, even if you're a seasoned bad weather driver. You should always leave plenty of space between your car and the one in front of you. Pay close attention to how you are driving and to other drivers on the road. You never know when another motorist may lose control and cause an accident. Stopping on snow and ice without skidding requires extra time and distance. If you have anti-lock brakes, press the pedal down firmly and hold it. If you do not have anti-lock brakes, do not slam on the brakes. Instead, it is very important to gently pump them in a consistent manner and stay calm and cool. Either way, give yourself plenty of room to stop.

8. If you find yourself in a skid, ease off of the gas and steer into the skid. This will bring the back end of the car in line with the front. By staying calm and cool and always knowing your surroundings, you can prevent an accident or being involved in an accident that someone else is causing.

9. Check the anti-freeze. It's easy to do with an inexpensive tester available at parts stores and at most department stores in the automotive section.

10. Examine the belts and hoses, look for checks and cracks in the belts. Also look for "soft" places and bulges in the hoses. If belts or hoses look suspect, change them. It's much easier to change them at the time and place of your choice rather than having to change one alongside a desolate road in the middle of the night in freezing weather.

11. Check the wiper blades. With winter approaching, it's essential to have fully operational blades. Sure they probably look ok, but examine them. Are they stiff, do they have any little chunks missing? Turn your lawn sprinkler on and let it sprinkle over your automobile for a few minutes or spray it with a hose. Then try the wipers. Are all the wiper speeds working? Is it removing sufficient water off of the windshield? If not, replace the wiper blades immediately. If you don't feel comfortable changing it yourself, take it to the shop and have it repaired. Poor visibility can cost you your life! Think about switching them out in the spring and in the fall. Remember, wiper blades are made out of rubber and what does rubber do? It rots! Change out windshield wiper blades at least twice a year or every 6,000 miles.

12. Make sure to have plenty of windshield wiper fluid for good visibility out of your windshield. Our driving decisions are based on visibility for our safety, our passengers' safety and for the safety of other drivers on the road. It is also a great idea to have extra windshield wiper fluid in your trunk or packed in your emergency road kit.

Kenny's Garage   Kenny Wallace

13. Now examine your tires. Look at the tread. Are there "dished out" places or spots where uneven wear is showing? If so, then not only do you need new tires, but you will also need to have the front end aligned. Measure the tread on your tires. Correct tire tread and pressure is crucial for driving in rain and snow.

14. Proper tire inflation is always needed for safer driving in any weather, but especially in poor traction conditions. Investing in a good set of snow tires is a wise investment. These tires can last you up to four winter seasons; depending on how many miles you put on your car per year. Always make sure to rotate and balance your tires every 5,000 miles. All you need to do is switch them out in the winter and spring, and then store them for the next winter. Snow tires will assist you in driving in snow or on slippery roads, especially if you do not have a four-wheel drive or all-wheel drive.

15. Check your brakes for wear. Worn brake parts can cause uneven braking and lots of trouble in the best of times. On snow and ice, it gets a lot worse. You may not notice any braking problem on dry pavement, but on ice and snow it can put you in the ditch or the hospital or both.

16. Now is the time to service your vehicle. Look in the owner's manual and follow the manufacturer's recommendations for service. They built the thing and they know when it needs to be serviced! It will make you and the vehicle a lot happier in the long run.

17. Don't forget the all-important tune-up. Most internal combustion engines will start and run in warm weather, but let it turn cold and damp and problems show up. Again, it's much easier to get the vehicle tuned-up and ready for winter at a time and place of your choice rather than letting the vehicle choose when it will or won't run properly. Vehicles often choose the most miserable places to tell you they need something repaired.

18. Use a moisture removal additive in your fuel, especially during the spring and fall when the temperature varies widely from day to day. This is available at most places that sell gasoline, as well as in the automotive section of parts stores and department stores. The best car care in the world won't prevent frozen fuel lines when moisture condenses in your fuel tank because the tank isn't full and the temperature has changed. I usually pour in a bottle every three to four fill-ups in the winter. Note: ask your car manufacturer recommendations or your mechanic.

19. This is also the time to get some ballast for your vehicle before the snow flies. Bags of sand or concrete blocks work very well to give that added traction needed for winter driving.

20. If you live in an area that gets a lot of snow and ice, tire chains may be a good investment for you.

Prepping Your Car for Summer

Whether you're preparing your car for winter or for summer, there are adjustments and inspections that will need to be made pertaining to seasonal change.

If you've been using snow tires, swap them out with your regular tires. Swapping your tires will give you a quieter, smoother ride.

Check your tire pressure to make sure it is at the correct level. You may want to adjust it for hotter operating conditions that we deal with in the summer. Also, having the proper air pressure will assure that you get better gas mileage and that your tires last longer.

Inspect the belts and hoses and have them replaced if need be.

Inspect the wiper blades, replace them if they are worn out, and always make sure you have plenty of windshield wiper fluid.

Bugs can be more of a nuisance in the summer. Keep your windshield clean and clear of them in order to stay safe on the road.

Because the engine's cooling system works harder in warm

Kenny's Garage   Kenny Wallace

weather, have the radiator and radiator hoses checked and ALWAYS maintain a proper level of engine coolant. 50% water to 50% antifreeze mix is perfect.

Of course, check all of your fluids yourself or have them checked by a qualified mechanic. Remember; always have your oil changed every 3,000 miles.

Please take time to make the inspections and adjustments that are necessary to assure a safe ride for you and other drivers on the road. This keeps your car's mechanical health as good as it can be.

Kenny's Garage   Kenny Wallace

What to Do After an Accident

Every day, thousands of drivers are involved in automobile accidents. I want to talk about the few steps that should be taken right after an accident:

1. Remember to remain calm and always have an emergency road kit in your car.

2. After an accident, make sure all drivers and passengers are safe. If someone needs medical attention, call 911 before doing anything else.

3. If the car is still operational, make sure to get it off of the road or freeway and place road flares around the scene to insure the safety of all parties involved, including other drivers on the road. There are over 3,000 deaths every year caused by cars broken down on the side of the road.

4. Make sure you exchange important information like names, addresses, phone numbers, and insurance information. If there were witnesses, get their information too.

5. Take photos of the accident to document all damage to your vehicle and the other vehicles involved.
If the law enforcement in your area no longer takes accident reports unless there is an injury, make sure you

file one with your local DMV.

Note: Having an auto accident can be extremely stressful and costly. Chances are you will be involved in one or more at some point in your life. Keep safety a priority.

How to Get the Most Value When Selling Your Car

Preparing to Sell your Car

Whether you are going to sell your car on your own or you are going to trade it in at a dealership for a new one, you will want to prepare it as much as you can in order to get the most money out of it. The newspaper is an obvious place to list your car, but listing it in an online marketplace can gain you a worldwide audience of buyers! You will also be able to post a bunch of photos of your ride.

For the exterior:
1. Make sure that your tires are in good shape and balanced.
2. Fill in the small scratches.
3. Give your car a good detail and use a shiny wax.
4. Shine your wheels or hubcaps.
5. Use a shiny tire dressing on your tires.
6. Clean your windshield and windows thoroughly inside and out.
7. Check all of your fluids and add to if necessary.

For the interior:
1. Vacuum it thoroughly, including carpets, seats and console.
2. Shampoo the carpets.
3. Clean all surfaces with an all-purpose cleaner.
4. Apply a good non-greasy dressing to the dash and other

vinyl surfaces.

5. Apply a non-greasy leather conditioner if you have leather seats.

6. Always check for change that gets lost in the seat cracks, might pay for lunch!

7. If there are small, inexpensive repairs that you can do on your own or have done, I strongly encourage you to do so. I love a favorite saying of people in the car business that we should all live by: "Spending $50 will get you $500 more."

Dents and Dings

I know a wise old saying: "It's not on the outside, but the inside that counts." However, if you want to make a good sale on your vehicle, paying attention to the outside is crucial. Here are two tricks of the trade I have always shared with friends and family in order to get those pesky dents and dings out of your car's exterior:

1. Use dry ice on a hot day.
To use dry ice to help get a dent out of your car, it needs to be done on a hot day to insure that the metal on the car is pliable and easy to work on. Simply take the dry ice (use a neoprene gloves so that the dry ice does not tear off skin from your hands) and place the ice on the dent. Move it around the area of the dent, and the extreme difference between the temperature of the ice and the car's metal will make the metal on your car expand outwards, popping out

the dent.

2. Use a household tool that has another unique major use. If you have not heard of this home remedy by now, it will probably make you chuckle. We are going to be using a necessity to any bathroom to get that ding out of your car. That's right, the old handy bathroom plunger. Makes sense when you think about it, but I bet you don't spend too much time sitting around thinking about your bathroom plunger.

If possible, put your car in the sunlight to heat up the area of the car's metal that has the dent or ding. This will make it easier to pop out.

Locate the area of the dent or ding and then simply put the plunger to the metal. Press in enough to feel that you have a good connection, and then when you think the plunger has successfully affixed itself to the metal and you have enough suction, simply pull the plunger out towards you. You may want to repeat this step several times until you are satisfied with the results.

Keep in mind that these techniques may not perfectly fix dents or dings, but they will get most of the problem popped out.

Kenny's Garage   Kenny Wallace

Filling in Small Scratches

It is not necessary to have your whole car painted, or even the entire panel painted, because you have a few scratches. Most of the time, you can fill in minor scratches to create a smooth, new-looking appearance.

Most people who fill in a scratch defer to the old bottle of paint and brush applicator that comes with the bottle. You can find them at most auto supply stores.

Over many years of working in the automotive industry, I've learned a few tricks of the trade. Here's a trick to fill those small scratches: You will need to buy a medical syringe with a small needle. You can usually find one at a medical supply house. In order to get the correct match for your car's paint, contact a body shop and give them the make, model, and year of your vehicle, or simply take it to them so that they can look at your car and give you the correct color.

Fill the syringe with the paint, and then carefully insert the needle's tip into the far end of the scratch. Release enough paint in order to fill in the scratch completely. Make sure you do not overfill the scratch, or you will have paint running over perfectly fine areas of the car.

Let the paint dry completely before washing the car. The benefit of this procedure is that you will be filling in the scratch and not painting over it.

Keeping Your Car's Resale Value
Let's discuss ways to keep your car's resale value as high as possible, so you will be able to get the most money out of it when you decide to sell it.

When first purchasing a car, always have in the back of your mind how its value will hold up for resale. Pick your car wisely.

Never toss maintenance records. Your potential buyer will want to review those to be assured that the car's maintenance has been performed on a timely basis.
Keep your car's color real. I do not suggest painting it turquoise, because when it comes time to sell it, you will limit the number of potential buyers. Besides, who wants to own a turquoise car?

Sometimes we cannot avoid eating in our car, but keep in mind that food and drink spills stain upholstery and carpeting, reducing the resale value. It's always a good idea to scotch guard your car's interior. This will keep those Kool-Aid stains from doing a tie-dye job on your seats.

Maintain your car inside and out by having regularly

scheduled maintenance and by giving it a thorough cleaning on a regular basis. It is also important if you have a leather interior to keep it conditioned with a good leather product.

When replacing your tires, you will do better in the long run if you purchase all four tires at the same time instead of buying two for the front and two for the rear at a later time. Also, keep your tires rotated and balanced to get the longest possible life out of them.

You can go the extra mile by adding a clear coat protector to your car's exterior surface. This will prevent premature aging and oxidation.

Keep in mind that all cars depreciate over time. Keep your expectations high, but keep it real when pricing your used car.

Applying a Carpet and Upholstery Protector to Your Car's Interior

Food spills and human stains have always been a nuisance. They stain the car's interior and cause the resale value to depreciate more than necessary. After trying a variety of Carpet and Upholstery Protector products over the years, I have narrowed down my favorites. I suggest you do your own research and find your favorite tried and true product. It is very easy to apply to the carpet and upholstery and will keep your car looking fresh and new.

First, vacuum and shampoo the car's interior carpets and upholstery, or, do this procedure as soon as you buy a new car before something accidentally spills on the interior.
To apply the product, simply spray it onto the surface. Do a small area at a time, and repeat the process throughout your entire vehicle

Let it dry for about four hours before stepping onto it or putting a floor mat onto the carpet.

Future stains will easily blot out with a damp cloth!
By spending approximately one hour, you will thank yourself over and over again for not having to drive around in a car with Kool-Aid stains, or other spills that haunt you every day. It will also prevent premature fading.

Applying a Clear Coat Protector to Your Car's Paint
By spending an hour or so applying a clear coat protector to your car's paint, you'll not only prevent oxidation and premature fading, but you'll also retain the resale value of your car, and keep the paint looking spiffy!

There is a wide selection of clear coat products on the market. My recommendation may not be your favorite, so research before you choose!

Kenny's Garage   Kenny Wallace

Things to Keep In Mind When Buying a Car

…Or a truck, or anything that has four wheels and a motor! My daily driver is a Lexus GS 350; this is the nicest car I have ever owned. I want to also mention that I have a 1963 Chevrolet, short bed, lowrider, fleetside pick-up truck that I have owned for quite a few years, and I have way too much money invested in it. I was born in 1963, so it is an awesome truck. It is what we call a restorod. A restorod means we took the chains off of the tailgate, and kept a lot of the old features, but we installed power brakes and power steering. It's also purple, and it has a great sound system. It has a Corvette fuel-injected motor in it and starts great all of the time. When I was looking for a motor to put into it, they asked me "Kenny, do you want a brand new motor or one where a guy flipped his Corvette the first ten miles that he owned it?" My response was, "Heck yeah, I'll take the ten mile Corvette motor!" I only had to pay $1500 for a Corvette fuel-injected motor with only ten miles on it. I have put over $80,000 into the truck, way too much money.

Kenny Schrader makes fun of me all of the time. He calls me a fool for having so much money invested in that truck. What I've learned is that anyone who buys a project truck like this pays for the entire restoration, as this truck has been taken down to the frame. There has been a massive amount of labor put into it. If I were to sell it, I might be lucky to get $25,000 for it. However, I will never sell this truck!

Car Buying Advice
A friend of mine was eager to own his first "step side." He hunted high and low for the perfect deal at the right price, and he found it. What a deal. What a beauty. "What's that funny smell?" his buddy asked. The seller replied, "carpet shampoo and a bit of fragrance." They snatched up this "good deal" and drove away. Later, they found out that the truck was rescued out of a lake, and the smell just got worse over time. They tried everything to get rid of that smell, and found putting boxes of kitty litter under the seat seemed to work somewhat. Buyer beware!

There is so much about our cars we don't even know! The biggest fear that people ask me about when buying a new car is mechanical issues. They don't know what is going on underneath the hood. Unfortunately, when they go in to buy the car, they haven't done enough shopping around or comparing. Research is hugely important when it comes to making this purchase, and the Internet is an incredible resource. Look at product reviews, resale values, and things like that.

Our cars are typically the second largest investment that we make, so we want to take very good care of them, not only for performance but also for longevity. We need to protect

Kenny's Garage — Kenny Wallace

that investment.

For years, it has been my good fortune to share helpful information with family, friends and consumers through television, radio and print media. This has often reduced fears that consumers typically have with regards to vehicles and has increased their confidence in proceeding with their next car purchase.

When shopping for a car, there are several key fundamentals that you as the buyer should focus on in order to insure that you're making the best purchase. First of all, you should establish a budget. This will enable you to narrow down your possible choices to those models in your price range. Secondly, as a buyer you should research the makes and models that you find appealing that fit within your budget parameters.

It has been published over and over by numerous sources that consumers make the final decision on price when purchasing the automobile, whether it is for their own use or for the use of their husband and family.

I also know that once we do "pull the trigger" on that car purchase we need to remember how serious it is to keep up regular maintenance on our vehicle in order to keep rolling down the street!

Kenny's Garage   Kenny Wallace

I always advise consumers to go out and test drive several makes and models to find the best fit for all of their needs. I have a favorite saying: "There's a butt for every seat." My choice may not be your exact choice because we all have different budgets, likes and dislikes when it comes to our car preferences.

I will, however, remind you to consider what makes and models have the best consumer ratings, resale values, safety ratings and also look for a great factory warranty.

You are also correct to consider the future maintenance cost and, of course, the gas mileage that can make or break your bank account. It would definitely be a wiser choice to buy a car that is slightly used in order to let someone else absorb the depreciation that goes along with a spanking brand new car.

When buying a new car look at the options that come standard. A lot of cars will come with standard options that other manufacturers will consider upgrades. If certain options are standard, that means it comes in the base price. If those options are an upgrade, they will charge you $2,000 for leather, $2,000 for a sunroof, etc. In other words, you're not going to have to pay extra for those options. I've sent a ton of people to Audi for this reason. If you buy an A6, it has a sunroof, alloy wheels, a sound system, and all for a great base price, whereas if you're looking at a comparable car, you're paying almost double for the same vehicle.

Also consider spending about $1,200 and invest in an extended warranty that will cover your car up to 100,000 miles on the odometer bumper to bumper.

Many manufacturers do offer an extended warranty that is of value whether you do or do not sell the car, and if you do sell the car your future buyer is going to be happy. But, nowadays a lot of manufacturers are giving 100,000-mile factory warranties on their products. Go in with the mindset of purchasing a particular car, but if you're not thrilled with what the warranty entails, maybe you should be looking at a different manufacturer, make and model. Much of your decision to buy a car should come down to what kind of warranty you will get on it.

Also, consider a two-wheel drive instead of a four-wheel drive if you live in a climate that does not require a four-wheel drive grip.

Options That May or May Not Suit Your Needs
All-Wheel Drive

It is always a smart decision to invest in an all-wheel drive vehicle if you live in an area that has significant weather issues (e.g. snow, heavy rain, etc.) not only for your personal safety but also for the safety of the passengers in your vehicle and other drivers on the road. Plus, this decision will usually result in lower premiums on the insurance coverage of your car.

4-Door Vehicle
If you have a family or about to start one, choose a four door vehicle for the obvious practical purposes of accessibility when putting the car seat in and out, and also the additional back seat space. It seems to me that when you load up the family for a road trip that it should be as painless as possible, even though it is much like a "troop movement."

Gas Mileage
It is not necessary to purchase a V8 engine to have a lot of get up and go. Today's four and six cylinder engines put out more than ample horsepower to get the speed you desire, plus you will realize better gas mileage.

Color Selection
When choosing a color, remember to pick one that will be desirable in a resale market, if and when you decide to sell the car. I do not suggest buying a turquoise car, because that decision will limit the number of potential buyers that would have an interest in your car. I would however, suggest one of the most popular colors for resale: black, silver, white or red.

Kenny's Garage Kenny Wallace

Extended Warranty
When purchasing an extended warranty, I would thoroughly research the warranty company and their financial stability. Many automobile manufacturers will reduce the cost of the extended warranty if you purchase it before the manufacturer's factory warranty expires.

Used Vehicle Mechanical Inspection
Have the car checked out by a qualified mechanic, or have the dealership from which you are purchasing it give you a detailed inspection report of the items that were inspected and/or repaired while in their possession. Or use the knowledge that you have learned here so far and inspect it yourself!

Understanding That Sticky Sticker Price
It is important to remember that creating a competitive environment, and time, are two of your greatest negotiating tools. If you can locate more than one car that fits your needs from multiple dealerships, work one dealership against the other in order to get a better deal and the price you need to fit your budget. I suggest telling the dealer that you would like to go home and think about the purchase and consider your options before accepting the final offer. Go home and give it a couple of days. They will definitely call you and make a better offer.

DO NOT BUY the first car you test drive. Simply say

"No." Shop around, and let them know you're shopping around. Give yourself time to make the right decision. When understanding the sticker price, the manufacturers always have a base price. They add to that price with options and add-ons.

Keep in mind that some manufacturers have options and add-ons that are already included in the base price. Due diligence always pays off, so put in the effort and research the exact make and model that you want, then test drive them all to see what fits your budget and your tastes the best. The warranty is also extremely important. It can keep you from going broke on car repairs in the future, so keep that in mind when making your final decision.

When buying those additional options on your car, the extended warranty, undercarriage protection, paint protection and all of the other add-ons that are offered it might be best for you to go ahead and roll them into the total financed price of the vehicle rather than taking large lumps of money out of your pocket.

I remember when I purchased my first new car; I shopped around, went from dealership to dealership, and then went home to think about it. That first evening, the dealerships started calling me and offering me incentives and better prices. I realized the best way to get the best price was to play one dealership against the other.

Kenny's Garage   Kenny Wallace

There is a limit to how much a dealer can take off the sticker price, so ask to see the invoice of the car. If you feel good about the final price, then make the purchase.

Used Car Shopping
When shopping for a used car, narrow down your search by deciding on the exact make and model that you're looking for and the budget that you've set for purchasing the car. When shopping for a good, dependable used car, there are key elements to examine before writing that check. I always inspect the car mechanically first. So roll up your sleeves and pop the hood. Lemons are much cheaper at the supermarket. No need to write a big check for one with four tires. Start by checking out the fluids and the condition of the visible belts and hoses.

When checking the oil, make sure that it has a honey brown color. If the oil is dark and goopy (it's a word, I swear), then the previous owner probably did not have regular oil changes performed. A potential engine issue may exist, so be aware.

When checking the transmission fluid, the fluid should have a rich red color to it, and should never feel gritty or grimy or like it has metal flakes in it. If it does, this might mean that the gears inside the transmission are grinding up, so be aware.

The brake fluid, power steering fluid, windshield washer fluid and coolant should be at proper levels. The belts and hoses should never look cracked or expanded like they are going to explode or break. Tires are important, so make sure that all four are in good condition and check the spare too.

Inside the vehicle, check out all the power options; mirrors, blinkers, headlights, taillights, brake lights, air conditioner, heater and of course, the stereo. Test-drive the car to see if it fits your liking, and if you want your mechanic to check it out, that's fine too!

Buying a used car can be tricky, but then again, keep in mind that it is a used car and not a new one, so expect that there will be repairs needed. Keep some money set aside for that.

Many dealers are pushing certified pre-owned vehicles on buyers, sometimes even more than they push new cars. Is this a good option?

Certified pre-owned cars are good cars. A car that is "certified" has been run through the dealer's service department and was "reconditioned," meaning they spent money putting on new brakes, adding tires, etc. They "certify" it, guaranteeing that it is a good product, plus you are getting an extended warranty.

Looking for Possible Paintwork

When purchasing a car that has had previous paintwork, do not assume that the car has had or will have a problem. You can take the car to a qualified, reputable body shop and have them determine if the repair was done properly, or you can look at the paintwork yourself.

Keep these tips in mind to determine if the paintwork was done properly:
The body shop will typically tape off the panels before painting them, so open the door jam and run your finger along the edge. If there is a ridge (we call it a tape line in the industry) this means that the panel was painted. Repeat this process for all of the panels, including the front fenders, underneath the hood, and also, check the deck lid.

You can also tell if the front fenders have been removed or replaced if the paint on the screws seems to be chipped off, if the screws do not align up properly, or if the gaps between the hood and fenders seem to be lopsided.

Another way you can tell is if there is over spray. This means that the body shop got a little paint spray on the moldings.

Most import cars have the VIN plates on all panels of the vehicle. If you see a panel that does not have the VIN plate, this could mean that the whole panel was replaced with an after-market one.

I have owned many cars in the past with previous paintwork, and of course have had accidents that have caused me to get parts of a car repaired and painted. Just because a car has had paintwork doesn't mean that you have to be leery of it. Also, you may be able to get a better deal when purchasing it.

You can also learn a lot about a vehicle's history by ordering a history report online from several different companies that specialize in this.

With this information, you should be able to buy the car with confidence and at a reduced price, especially if it's been in a previous accident.

What about Car Insurance?
Make sure you carry liability, because you don't want to lose your license. A friend of mine was not carrying liability. He had a one-time ticket and lost his driver's license privileges and had his license suspended for a year. Some states are even stricter, so it's very important to have liability coverage.

Kenny's Garage — Kenny Wallace

It might cost a bit more, but get a rental car option on your insurance. If you wreck your car, this ensures you'll have a rental car.

Also, shop around. There are so many competing car insurance companies out there today it's insane. If you look at the commercials on television, they're as competitive as beer commercials. Keep looking until you find a policy you can afford that suits all of your needs.

How-To Segments

I was eight years old when I started working on cars. I grew up in a racing family; my dad Russ Wallace and my brothers Rusty and Mike, we raced, we were as redneck as you could get. I am very proud to be a Missouri Redneck.

We went to bed without taking showers. We ate bologna and cheese sandwiches. We lived in the garage, literally. I remember one time looking at my bed sheets and you could see where I slept because it was dirty, and the rest of the sheets were clean. I remember my sixth grade teacher Ms. Grab. She said, "Kenny can I talk to you?" "I said, "Yes, Ms. Grab." She said, "Honey, you are a great boy, but you smell like a shop." I loved working in that shop until midnight every night. I would not take a shower, but just wash my arms and hands and never really realized just how bad I must have smelled.

I lived in that shop from the time I was six years old, and my job was to work on my Dad's dirt car. At that time, we used old drum brakes, not disc brakes. My job was to take the hubs off and use the wire brush to clean them and then blow them out to get them ready for the next race. I did three things; I changed the gears, cleaned the brakes and changed the tires.

Kenny's Garage — Kenny Wallace

How ironic that my teacher Ms. Grab had a relative that was a racecar driver, Roger Grab. I did not put two and two together until later that my teacher was related to Roger Grab the racecar driver. Roger was a wild guy; he drove a green Chevelle with the number thirteen. In racing, everything he did was unlucky. He drove a green car, and had the number thirteen on it, so the announcer would say, "Here he comes, the mean green, unlucky thirteen machine, Roger Grab!"

How to Change Your Oil

For this task, you will need the following parts: new engine oil, new oil filter.

You will also need the following tools: oil filter wrench, set of wrenches, oil drain pan, jack stands or ramps, a fender cover and shop towels.

Let's start with the oil change. Run your vehicle for a few minutes to make sure the engine oil will thoroughly drain. Position your vehicle safely on a lift or on jack stands. Turn the engine off, and remove the oil fill cap, hence allowing for better suction when removing the old engine oil.

Use a wrench to remove the oil drain plug. Use a drain pan to collect all of the old oil as it comes out of the reservoir. Next, remove the engine oil filter by using an oil filter wrench. Make sure that you remove the oil filter gasket with the oil filter.

Install the new engine oil filter by using your hand and twisting clockwise. Reinstall the drain plug. It will help to apply a light coat of old oil on the oil filter gasket to keep it from cracking under high vehicle temperatures.

Now, fill the vehicle engine with the manufacturer's recommended oil.

You can then start the engine, to circulate the oil, and then turn it off to check your oil levels.

How to Switch Out Your Spark Plugs
For this task, you will need the following part: spark plugs. You will also need the following tools: screwdrivers, sockets and a ratchet, socket extension, spark plug socket, spark plug gapping tool.

Now we will take a look at how to perform a spark plug and spark plug wire change. First, gain access to the spark plug wires. On some vehicles, they may be hidden under plastic covers.

Mark the plug wires for installation reference. Then remove all the spark plugs and replace them with new ones. Each vehicle's firing order is very specific and must be correct. Either mark each wire or do them one by one.

Kenny's Garage					Kenny Wallace

When removing and replacing spark plug wires, it is strongly recommended to lay out the new wires, and match them to the corresponding length wires already installed on the engine. This process is best accomplished by replacing each wire one by one.

Be careful not to connect the wrong spark plug to the wrong terminal on the distributor cap. This will cause the wrong cylinder to fire at the wrong time and the vehicle will not run correctly.

How to Change Your Air Filter
For this task, you will need the following part: new air filter.
You will also need the following tools: screwdriver.

Locate the air filter box inside the engine compartment.

The air cleaner assembly commonly looks like a plastic box.

Release the clips or remove the screws that hold the cover on the filter box, and remove the cover.

Next, simply remove the old air filter. If the filter is clogged with dirt or debris, it will need to be replaced. Also inspect the box assembly, and remove any dirt or leaves that may be sitting inside.

To replace, simply install the new air filter into the filter box assembly.

Replace the cover and install the clamps or tighten the screws to secure the cover. Make sure your air filter box is completely sealed to protect it from dirt and debris. Finally, inspect the air intake tube and all vacuum lines to ensure they are all properly attached.

How to Check Belts
For this task, you will need the following parts: a new belt. You will also need the following tools: wrench, 3/8" ratchet and set of sockets.

Now we will look at checking your belts. Open the hood and locate either your Serpentine belt, or your V-belts.

Check the belts carefully for any cracks in the grooves, or any splitting of the belt material. You should always replace your belts at recommended intervals.

Loosen the tension from the pulley and remove the old belt. Locate the adjustment fastener and loosen it. Then move the tension pulley far enough away from the belt to allow you to remove it.

Now install the new belt, making sure it is properly seated in the pulley groove or grooves. Make sure you have the right belt size before installing. Compare it to the old one; it should be the same shape and size.

Make sure your belt or belts are positioned correctly and that the tension pulley is tight and in place. The tension on the belts must be correct so they do not slip off when the vehicle is running.

How to Switch Out Your Distributor Cap
For this task, you will need the following parts: distributor cap and rotor.
You will also need the following tools: sockets, ratchet, and a screwdriver.

Open the hood and locate the vehicle's distributor cap within the engine compartment.

Loosen the clips that hold the cap to the distributor housing and inspect under the cap for carbon build-up. Carbon build-up will look like dirt tracking between the inner terminals. If you notice any carbon, you will need to replace the distributor cap.

Go ahead and loosen the clips that hold the cap to the distributor housing. Remove the old distributor cap with the plug wires still attached, and set it aside for now.

Replace the old rotor with its new replacement piece. Then, install the new distributor cap in the same position as the old one.

Starting with the wire closest to the #1 plug indicator on the cap, remove and reinstall the wires from the old cap to the new one, in a clockwise rotation. Avoid randomly connecting plug wires.

Now you can start the vehicle and make sure that it starts and runs smoothly, that there are no misfires or backfires occurring.

How to Talk Kenny Schrader into Teaching You How to Drive Dirt Car

My dear friend Kenny Schrader, I kept aggravating him. I said, "Schrader, teach me how to drive a dirt car." After months of aggravating him, and by this time I was 39 years old, he said, "Why do you want to learn how to drive a dirt car so bad?" I said, "All I have ever done is race asphalt." My first race win ever was in 1982 in Springfield, Illinois at the Springfield Fairgrounds. I did not race again until 1986 because I got busy with my brother Mike and Rusty's racing career working as a mechanic. Schrader kept asking me why I wanted to run dirt so bad and I told him that Mario Andretti, A.J. Foyt, those guys did it all. I told him I have raced hundreds of NASCAR races and love the road courses in NASCAR, I have run two Daytona 24 hour races in GT Class, and it is really important to me to race dirt.

Schrader got me hooked up on modified dirt and then super late model dirt. However, what got me really addicted was in 2005, I won the first ever Tony Stewart's Prelude to a Dream at Eldora Speedway. Finishing second was Tony Stewart, third was Dave Blaney. I won that race and Tony came running up to victory lane because he was second, and he said, "What was that all about?"...I said, "I have no idea, the car just handled so good." So I always tease Schrader now that after winning that Prelude to a Dream in 2005 he cost me two million dollars because I bought land, built my shop, bought my hauler, and employed an employee for nine years now. But seriously, it has been the best thing that has ever happened in my life besides marrying my wife, Kim. Dirt racing has saved me. I love it. Racing dirt has saved my soul. It is hard to stop racing, I can run dirt easily until I am 60 years old because the races are only 50 laps long. Schrader and I will run dirt until we can't get into the car anymore.

Schrader and I race dirt a lot together but we will go several months without racing each other. Schrader has more cars than I do, so he can run more divisions like IMCA. I run a lot of UMP races. Schrader ventures off more on the West Coast and I stay more in the Midwest.

How to Inspect and Adjust Misaligned Headlights

To test and adjust your headlights, you will need a roll of masking tape, a wall, a tape measure, screwdriver, and a flashlight.

The first thing you want to do is park your car on a level grade, facing a wall. Ideally, the wall should be about 25 feet away from the front of your car.

With a tape measure, measure the distance from the ground to the center of your headlight lens. Also measure the distance between the two headlights.

Now, measure the same distance on the wall from the ground up, and apply a horizontal strip of masking tape exactly four inches below that mark.

Turn on the headlights and set them to low beam. When you see the lights shine on the wall, the top of the headlight beam should be lined up with the taped line.

If you discover your headlights to be out of alignment, it will be necessary to adjust them for optimal visibility while driving at night.

Locate the headlight vertical adjustment screw. Using a screwdriver, adjust vertically so the top cutoff of the

Kenny's Garage　　　　　　　　　　Kenny Wallace

headlight beam is at the top of the tapeline.

Locate the headlight horizontal adjustment screw. Adjust horizontally to position the beams straight ahead. To ensure proper headlight adjustment, the measurement between the headlight lenses and the beams on the wall should be equal.

How to Replace a Headlamp
Instead of taking your car to a mechanic when you have a bulb that is out, you can replace it yourself with a few simple steps.

First, determine the correct size bulb that you will need. You can either call your vehicle's manufacturer or go to your local auto parts store and give them the year, make and model of your car, and they will tell you the exact bulb you will need.

For this task, you will need a replacement headlamp bulb. Check the vehicle's user manual to find the appropriate size. You may also need screwdrivers and/or sockets and a ratchet.

Turn on the headlights from the steering wheel controls to confirm which bulb is out. Then, turn the lights back off. Open the hood, and find the headlamp assembly, which can be accessed from the back of the headlight in the engine compartment. Make sure the hood is propped up securely while the work is being done.

Disconnect the wiring harness, and replace the old headlamp bulb with the new one.

Repeat the previous step on the opposite side of the vehicle, even if that bulb is not burned out yet.

Before putting the whole apparatus back together, turn on the headlights to see if all of the bulbs are working properly and to confirm that the problem is fixed. Reassemble everything in the exact reverse steps that you used to get it apart.

Knowing how to do this on your own will not only give you a feeling of confidence when working on your vehicle, it will also prove how easy it is to do small repairs, and will save you money in the long run.

How to Replace a Brake Light Bulb
For this task you will need a new brake light bulb. You will also need a pocket screwdriver, a ¼" ratchet and a set of sockets.

Turn your key to the on position and press down on the brake pedal. Have an assistant inspect your taillights to determine which bulb is out.

Kenny's Garage   Kenny Wallace

Remove the lens assembly and then remove the wiring harness from the lens assembly. Disconnect the brake light bulb from the wiring harness. Install the new brake light bulb.

Reconnect the wiring harness to the lens assembly. Re-install the lens assembly.

Check your work by pressing the brake pedal (with the key turned on) and have an assistant check the light.

How to Replace a Turn Signal Bulb
For this task, you will need the correct bulb for your vehicle. The tools required for this job are a pocket screwdriver, 1/4" ratchet and a set of sockets.

Place the ignition key in the on position.

Activate your turn signal switch. When one of the turn signal bulbs burns out, the remaining bulbs will flash faster than normal.

Locate the burned out turn signal bulb.

Turn the ignition key to the off position.

Gain access to the turn signal bulb. Most turn signal bulbs are accessible through the back of the headlight and tail light assemblies. The turn signal bulb is either held in with a retainer clip or twisted on. Replace the bulb socket if damaged.

Remove the turn signal bulb harness from the lens assembly.

Disconnect the turn signal bulb from the harness.
Install the new turn signal bulb.

Reconnect the harness to the lens assembly.

Apply the turn signal to verify that the turn signal bulb is functioning properly.

How to Replace a Headlight Switch
For this task, you will need a replacement headlight switch that matches the broken one.
You will also need a screwdriver, a pocket screwdriver, a digital multi-meter and an interior trim tool.

Turn the ignition key to the on position so that all interior accessories are powered.

Turn the headlight switch to the on position, the high beam position and the fog light position to see if they illuminate. Check the headlight fuse and bulbs first, just to make sure they are working properly.

Next, pull out the headlight switch, and check for power and ground to the switch using a digital multi-meter. If the switch has the appropriate power and ground needed, then replacing the switch will fix the problem.

To replace it, simply disconnect the switch from the wiring connection, and install the new switch.

Turn the new headlight switch to the on position to check that the lights are illuminating and to verify the repair.

How to Replace a Blown Fuse
An electrical failure in your vehicle is most likely (but not always) due to a blown fuse. So it should be the first thing that you check.

The first step is to look at your owner's manual; it will help you to locate the fuse box and tell you how to access it.

To replace a fuse, you will need new fuses. You will also need your vehicle owner's manual, a test light, pocket screwdriver, flashlight, and a fuse puller.

First, identify the electrical component that is not working. Then, using your owner's manual, locate the fuse box. Usually, you can find it under the dash, or within the engine compartment.

Locate the fuse to the component that is not working. Most fuse panels are clearly labeled. If the panel is not labeled, you will have to test each fuse to locate the affected circuit. Now inspect the wire inside the fuse to see if it is broken (blown). If you are unable to tell if the fuse is blown, use a test light to test for voltage on both sides of the fuse. If there is voltage on one side only, the fuse is blown.

Using a fuse puller or tweezers, remove the old fuse, some vehicles supply a fuse puller in the fuse box.

The most critical element to replacing a blown fuse is using the exact same amperage as indicated in the owner's manual. If you use a different amperage fuse, you risk either blowing the fuse again or damaging the equipment the fuse is designed to protect.

The fuse will plug straight back into the fuse box and usually fit into place with a little pressure from your fingertip.

With the new fuse installed, you are ready to test the electrical component that was not working. And now, it is!

Kenny's Garage					Kenny Wallace

How to Replace a Starter

For this task, you will need the following parts: replacement starter; possible replacement flywheel, starter solenoid, and battery cables.

You will also need the following tools: rubber mallet, set of wrenches, 3/8" ratchet, set of sockets. ½" ratchet.

Open the vehicle's hood and locate the starter. If it is easier to see and touch the starter from the bottom, you will need to secure your vehicle on jack stands to inspect the starter's condition. Always make sure the hood shocks can fully support the weight, so that it does not close on you while working. Using a hood prop can securely hold it up in place.

Disconnect the negative battery cable, cover it with a towel and place it away from the battery post.

Next, mark the starter wires for installation reference. Remove the electrical wires that are attached to the starter.

Remove the starter.
Attach a ½ inch ratchet (with socket) to the harmonic balancer bolt at the front of the engine. Have an assistant turn the engine clockwise while you inspect the flywheel teeth with a flashlight. If any teeth are missing, cracked or chipped, you should replace the flywheel now.
Install the new starter.

Next, reconnect any electrical wires that may have been removed from the starter.

Secure the battery's negative cable back onto the post.

Finally, start the vehicle to verify the repair.

How to Replace a Water Pump
The parts you will need for this task are a water pump, water pump gasket, sealant and 50/50 mix of coolant and distilled water. The tools you will need for this project are a 3/8" drive ratchet, set of sockets, cooling system pressure tester, screwdriver, radiator hook tool, needle nose pliers, gasket scraper.

With the engine off and cold, open the hood and locate the vehicle's water pump. Before removing the radiator cap, squeeze the upper radiator hose to verify that the cooling system is not pressurized.

Remove the radiator cap.

Install cooling system pressure tester. Apply the pressure indicated on the radiator cap or in the owner's manual. Inspect cooling system components for leaks.

Place a drain pan under the radiator. Open drain valve or remove the lower radiator hose to drain cooling system.

Kenny's Garage Kenny Wallace

Depending on the vehicle you may need to lift the vehicle to gain access to the lower radiator hose.

Remove the drive belts or serpentine belt.

Remove any hoses connected to water pump.

Unbolt water pump from engine. Remove the water pump. Using a gasket scraper, clean the mating surface on the engine block.

Install new water pump and new gasket. Tighten bolts to manufacturer's specifications. You may want to use a light bead of silicone designed for water pumps.

Re-install any hoses and belts that were removed.

Re-install drain plug or lower radiator hose. Squeeze the radiator hose. If it feels soft you may want to replace the hose at this time. Always use new hose clamps.

Refill radiator with a 50/50 mix of coolant and distilled water. Then pressure test the cooling system and check for leaks.

Fill overflow reservoir with same mixture.

Leave the radiator cap off, start engine and let it idle. You should see the system "burping" bubbles of air. Refill the radiator to the top. Most air is expelled after a couple minutes of idling. Be careful of the hot fluid.
Install radiator cap.

Road test the vehicle. Keep an eye on the engine temperature gauge. If the vehicle runs hot, there still might be an air pocket in the cooling system. The cooling system should be topped off after the vehicle has fully cooled down.

How to Replace an Alternator
In order to inspect and replace your alternator, you will need a new alternator.
You will also need a digital multi-meter, a set of sockets and ratchet, a small pry bar or screwdriver, and combination wrenches.

First, open the hood and locate your battery. Use the digital multi-meter to check the battery voltage. Dead batteries usually have less than 12 volts, not enough power to start most cars. Make sure you have a fully charged or new battery to verify the alternator is bad. A new battery should read about 12.6 volts with the engine off, and 13.5-14.5 volts with the engine running.

Kenny's Garage   Kenny Wallace

If the battery's voltage does not increase to 13.5 to 14.5 volts, while the engine is running, then you will need to replace the alternator.

With an open-end wrench, disconnect the battery's negative cable. Do not allow the cable to come into contact with the negative terminal while working on the vehicle. To prevent this from happening, wrap the cable in a shop towel and pull it away from the terminal.

Next, locate the alternator, usually at the front of the engine compartment. You will want to disconnect the power and ground wires on the back of the alternator, paying close attention to where each wire connects. Then, disconnect the wiring harness connector.

Loosen the alternator bracket bolts and alternator adjusting bolts (or alternator belt tension) and remove the alternator drive belt.

With the right-sized socket and ratchet, remove the alternator mounting bolts, spacer (if equipped), adjusting bolt, lower pivot bolt (if equipped), and then remove the alternator.

Now you are ready to install the new alternator. You will want to do the exact steps in reverse order. Install the alternator mounting bolts, spacer (if equipped), adjusting bolt, and lower pivot bolt (if equipped).

Install the alternator belt. Make sure the belt is fully seated in the groove of the pulleys, and pull the alternator until the belt is tight.

Tighten the alternator mounting bolts while gently moving the alternator unit to achieve proper belt tension.

Reinstall the power and ground wires to the alternator and install the wiring harness connector.

It is a good idea to push down in the middle of the alternator belt to check the tension. If it moves more than half an inch, it is too loose, and you will need to adjust it tighter before continuing.

Now that the alternator belt has been installed and adjusted, you will want to reconnect the battery cable. Start your engine and check the battery voltage to verify proper alternator charging.

Finally, turn off the engine and recheck the alternator belt tension. Readjust if necessary.

How to Replace the Alternator Belt
In order to inspect and replace the alternator belt, you will need a new alternator belt.

Kenny's Garage   Kenny Wallace

You will also need a flashlight, an inspection mirror, an impact gun, a screwdriver, and flare nut wrenches.

First, disconnect the negative battery cable and wrap it in a shop towel to prevent it from touching the terminal.

Next, locate the alternator belt near the front of the engine. Inspect the belt carefully. I would recommend twisting the belt over to check the underside for glazing, cracks, and other damage. Check for oil or any place the belt is wet.

You will probably want to check the belt tension as well.

Try pushing down in the middle section of the belt. If there is more than half an inch of tension, you will want to tighten the belt.

In order to replace the belt, loosen the alternator mounting bolts using the proper sized socket and ratchet or a combination wrench. Now you will be able to move the alternator inward so that you can loosen the belt. If you cannot move the alternator yourself, try using a small pry bar.

Remove the old belt by sliding it right off the pulley. Then simply install the new belt in reverse order. Make sure the belt is fully seated in the groove of the pulleys.

Pull the alternator until the belt is tight. Tighten the mounting bolts while gently moving the alternator unit to achieve proper belt tension. You will want to re-check the belt tension, and adjust if necessary.

Finally, start your engine. If you have replaced the belt properly, you will not hear anymore chirping or squealing.

How to Replace a Fog Light Assembly
For this task, you will need a new fog light assembly. You will also need the following tools: pocket screwdriver and a ¼ ratchet and set of sockets.

If the fog light assembly is damaged, you will need to locate the fog light assembly retaining bolts, usually located under and behind the front bumper.

Go ahead and remove the fog light assembly retaining bolts and disconnect the fog light assembly connectors from the wiring harness.

Next, remove the fog light assembly from the vehicle. Install the new fog light assembly into the vehicle.

Now, tighten the fog light assembly retaining bolts and reconnect the fog light assembly connectors to the wiring harness.

Kenny's Garage   Kenny Wallace

Turn on the fog lights to verify your repairs have been made.

How to Jumpstart a Car

If you are not lucky enough to have a jump-box, you will need to borrow a friend's car in order to jump-start your weak or dead battery. If your battery is low on water, simply pop off the cover or covers and check the level. You should be able to see the water level close to the top. If you are having a problem, it may be your battery cables. If there is corrosion on the connecters, the power from the battery will be altered. To get the corrosion off of the connectors, you will need to use a wire tool or wire brush. An easy quick fix is to use a can of cola. Pour the soda over the connectors and it will literally eat the corrosion off the connectors.

The owner's manual from your vehicle should explain how to use jumper cables, as the sequence in which you proceed is very important. The following steps should only be used as a guide.

When jump-starting your car, make sure that both car hoods are securely propped open for safety. Check that the batteries of both vehicles are the same voltage.

Make sure that the vehicles are not touching. For safety, check that both vehicles are in Park, the emergency brakes are engaged, and both hoods are propped open securely. Switch off both engines and all the electronics (except the rescue vehicle's hazard lights).

You will need to have the negative to the positive clamp attached onto the cable so they don't cross until you affix the first clamp to the proper terminal…unless you like fireworks! The terminals are marked so you can see what you are doing. Then affix the second clamp to the proper terminal.

Note: Black is for the negative and red is for the positive. You will need to repeat the same steps on the other car that will be giving you the juice you need to get your car started. Let the two cars sit for at least a minute. You can also rev the idle in the assisting car in order to get quicker voltage to your dead or weak battery. Try starting your car. If it is having a hard time, let it sit for a few minutes before trying again.

I would recommend, even after you have gotten your car started, to keep the battery connection on for a few more minutes to assure you get enough voltage to keep your car running; at least until you can get it to the shop to determine the exact problem. Repeat the same procedure when you are unhooking the cables. You will want to affix the first clamp to the cable to avoid sparks and simply repeat the same steps to unhook the other car.

Remove the jumper cables in the reverse order as you connected them starting with the one connected to the engine block or vehicle frame. When connecting or removing the cables, do not allow the red and black clips to touch each other, or the red lead to come into contact with the vehicle body. This could cause a spark or shock.

Once the dead battery is started, drive to your local shop for testing. Normal driving of the vehicle will not restore the battery to a reliable level of charge. The battery will need to be charged over a 24-hour period.

It is recommended that you have your battery tested every time you go to your mechanic for service.
Keep in mind that you may need to buy a new battery. It could possibly be the alternator that has gone bad. When this happens, it interrupts the voltage that keeps your car running.

How to Install a Battery
Once you or your qualified mechanic has determined that you need a new battery, you will need to find out exactly what type of battery is required.

There are many different brands available in the market, so if you prefer to do research, that's fine. Choose the one that you feel comfortable with that will fit your make, model and the year of your vehicle.

First, you will need to unhook the battery cables, making sure they do not touch each other.

Most cars have the battery braced. To install the battery, you must dismount it and pull it out. Make sure that the new battery you are about to install never touches the concrete while you are working because this can drain the power out of the battery.

When installing the new battery, remember that red goes with red and black goes with black, red is positive and black is negative.

Now let's install the new battery. Put it in its place attaching the cables one at a time, tighten them down, and then secure the entire battery into the bracket.

Used batteries, or refurbished batteries, are usually fine. I have purchased several of these in the past, and I was completely satisfied with them, so I definitely would recommend purchasing one, especially if you buy it from a store that offers you a warranty on the battery.

Kenny's Garage　　　　　　　　　　　Kenny Wallace

How to Replace Door Weather Stripping

For this task, you will need the following parts: door weather stripping and weather strip adhesive.

You will also need the following tools: interior trim tool, hose and water, weather stripping adhesive and a flashlight.

Have an assistant sit inside the car, and shut the door. From the outside, apply a stream of water to the top of the door. If water leaks inside, you will need to replace the weather stripping.

You need to use an interior trim tool to remove any interior trim panels that retain the door's weather stripping.

Now go ahead and remove the weather stripping from the door, being careful not to damage the interior.

Next, clean the old adhesive off the door trim-mounting surface. Then apply new adhesive to the mounting surface or weather stripping.

Install the new weather stripping, applying firm pressure in the middle, working your way out. Do not let the adhesive sit for more than 30 seconds before applying the weather stripping, or it will dry and not stick properly.

Now, apply another stream of water to the top of the door, and have your assistant verify the repair.

Kenny's Garage   Kenny Wallace

How to Replace a Window Regulator

For this task, you will need the following parts: window regulator; possible door panel retaining clips, window lift motor, and window guide.

You will also need the following tools: screwdrivers and/or set of sockets and a 3/8" ratchet, interior panel removal tool.

First, locate the power window fuse and verify that it is not blown. If the fuse is not blown, proceed to step two. If the fuse is blown, it will need to be replaced. Continue further inspections if the window remains non-functional after fuse replacement. You may need to locate the power window fuse by referring to the owner's manual.

Next, remove the door panel by removing the handles and switches. It is required to unscrew or unclip the panel. Refer to the vehicle specific service manual if available. There are several fragile plastic clips and hidden screws on the door panel that will break if removed improperly.

Inspect the window regulator assembly. Check for binding or damaged wiring.

Then, remove the vapor barrier.

Disconnect the glass from window regulator.

Kenny's Garage   Kenny Wallace

Next, tape the glass to doorframe. The glass should not require removal. Tape the glass out of the way to allow access to the window regulator and window lift motor assembly.

Disconnect the electrical connector from the window motor.

Then, remove the window regulator mounting bolts. Slide the window regulator out through the interior access opening of the door.
Install the new window regulator and tighten the mounting bolts.

Reconnect the electrical connector to the window motor.
Install the window back onto the window regulator.
Finally, re-install the vapor barrier, the door trim panel and handles/switches.

Remember to test the power window for proper operation by rolling the window up and down in complete cycles. After re-installing a window lift motor and regulator, it may be necessary to re-program it following the manufacturer's specific instructions. Not following or performing this step may result in improper power window function.

How to Replace the Cabin Air Filter

For this task, you will need the following parts: a new cabin air filter.

You will also need the following tools: screwdrivers and/or sockets and a ratchet.

You will probably want to refer to your car's manual for the specific location of your cabin air filter. Some are within the engine compartment, and some are in the dash. Some vehicles have more than one, and you should replace both if that is the case.

Loosen the air filter box and inspect the cabin air filter for debris, dirt, leaves, and other objects that are obstructing the path of air entering the cabin.

Remove the old filter and clean the filter box thoroughly.

Now install the new filter, and secure the box.

Run the A/C with the doors closed to test your work.

How to Inspect the A/C Compressor

In order to inspect the A/C compressor, you will need a flashlight and an inspection mirror. This inspection will only take a couple of minutes to perform.

First, open the hood and locate your vehicle's A/C

compressor. It is a good idea to take the key out of the ignition and allow the engine to cool completely to prevent burns or injury. If your A/C compressor is hard to access, try using your flashlight and mirror.

The next step, after you locate the compressor, is to check the A/C belt. If the belt is missing, try to spin the A/C compressor by hand to verify the compressor is frozen. If the A/C compressor is locked up, or frozen, it will need replacing.

How to Inspect the A/C Condenser
In order to inspect the A/C condenser, you will need a flashlight and an inspection mirror. This inspection will only take a couple of minutes to perform.

The first step is to locate the condenser, usually found near the radiator. Inspect the condenser carefully for cracks that would lead to leaking.

The most common cause for a cracked condenser is a rock or object striking the part while you are driving.

How to Inspect the A/C Line or Hose
In order to inspect the A/C lines and hoses, you will need a flashlight and an inspection mirror.

Open the hood and locate the A/C lines or hoses, usually

found near the radiator. Always be sure to remove the key from the ignition, and allow the engine to cool completely prior to working on your vehicle to prevent burns or injury. Carefully inspect the lines or hoses for any cracks or possible kinks. Even the smallest crack will allow leakage, so do this carefully with a flashlight.

You will also want to carefully check the hose fittings and mounting bracket locations for wear and leaks.

How to Inspect the A/C System
To inspect the A/C system, you will need a flashlight and an inspection mirror. It should not take you long to inspect the various parts of the A/C system to determine the problem.

Within the engine compartment, locate the A/C lines and hoses. Inspect the lines or hoses very carefully for cracks or kinks that may be causing a leak. Also, be sure to check the hose fittings and mounting bracket locations for any wear and tear that may cause leaks. If the line or hose feels or looks wet, it's a good bet its leaking refrigerant or oil.
Next, take a look at the A/C condenser. Check carefully for any cracks that may cause leaking. Additionally, check the A/C line connection at the A/C condenser as well.
Thirdly, you will want to inspect the A/C evaporator for any cracks that could lead to leaks.

Fourth, check out the A/C compressor. Make sure it is free from any damage that may contribute to the problem.

If you notice any of the A/C components that are damaged or leaking, you will need to replace them. Any leak in the system will cause a drop in refrigerant levels and will prevent you're A/C from blowing cold air. Not good on a hot day! Remember, A/C systems require special equipment that only Certified Technicians are qualified to handle. Please consult a professional before attempting to replace any part of your A/C system.

How to Inspect the A/C Heater Blower
To inspect the A/C heater blower, you will need: a flashlight, a 3/8" drive ratchet, a set of sockets, a pocket screwdriver, a power probe or jumper wires and a volt meter.

First, with a flashlight, locate the A/C heater blower. This is usually found beneath the dash, usually on the passenger side behind the glove box.

Second, remove the A/C heater blower. To do this, disconnect the heater blower's electrical connector and mounting bolts. This will allow you to remove the box and the blower motor assembly. Then take out the A/C heater blower motor. Some heater blowers may not be accessible without removing the dash, and may require a different approach for inspecting and testing.

The next step is to bench test the heater blower. To do this, apply B+ and ground to test the heater blower. Does the fan spin? Are any fan fins broken?

If you have discovered any broken fins on the fan, or if you were unable to make the fan spin by applying a B+ and ground, then you can be sure the A/C heater blower fan is broken and will need replacing.

How to Replace the A/C Heater Blower
To replace the A/C heater blower in your vehicle, you will need an A/C heater blower assembly.
You will also require the following tools: a flashlight, a 3/8" drive ratchet, a set of sockets, a set of wrenches, a screwdriver, and a digital multimeter.

First, remove any dash components to gain access to the A/C heater blower. Disconnect the heater blower's electrical connector and mounting bolts. Remove the box and the blower motor assembly.

Remove the motor from the box assembly. Install the new A/C heater blower motor into the box and reassemble the necessary parts. Then mount it back into its original position.

Reconnect the blower motor electrical connector. Re-install the dash components.

Turn on the heating and A/C system and verify that the blower motor operates at all speeds and that the system produces hot air when in the heat position, and cold air when in the A/C position.

How to Replace the Heater Core Hoses

For this task, you will need replacement heater hoses, coolant and possibly replacement hose clamps and a gasket. You will also need a ratchet, sockets, a screwdriver, a coolant pressure tester, a drain pan and hose clamp pliers. Open the hood and inspect the heater core hoses for signs of leaking. Sometimes, pressure testing the system can help locate exactly where the leak is coming from. Allow the engine to cool down before removing any of the cooling system components.

Place a drain pan under the radiator drain valve. Open the valve and drain the coolant into the pan.

Loosen the hose clamps and remove the leaking heater hose.

Install the new hose and refill the cooling system with a 50/50 mixture of coolant and distilled water. Pressure-test the cooling system and check for leaks.

Run the engine to remove trapped air from the cooling system. Let the engine cool down again before re-checking the coolant level. Add coolant if necessary.

Re-install the radiator cap, close the engine compartment hood, and test-drive the vehicle to verify the repair.

How to Replace the Upper Radiator Hose
For this task, you will need the following part: upper radiator hose.
You will also need the following tools: cooling system pressure tester, screwdriver, radiator hook tool and needle nose pliers.

Open the hood and locate the radiator. Carefully inspect the upper and lower radiator hoses for any wear and tear. Be sure the engine is off and cool before doing this.

To test the hoses further, attach a pressure tester to the radiator and apply the amount of pressure indicated on the radiator cap. Inspect the hoses for leaks. If a hose is leaking, you will need to replace it.

Place a drain pan under the radiator drain valve. Open the drain valve and drain the cooling system.

Kenny's Garage   Kenny Wallace

Next, remove the upper radiator hose clamps. Now remove the upper radiator hose.

Install the hose clamps on the new radiator hose. I install the new hose and place the clamps over the hose ends. Fill your radiator and overflow tank with a 50/50 mixture of coolant and distilled water. Test-drive your vehicle to verify the repair.

How to Replace the Transmission Cooler Lines
For this task, you will need replacement transmission fluid lines and transmission fluid.
You will also need a floor jack, jack stands, a set of sockets and ratchet, a flash light, a mirror, a can of brake cleaner, a drain pan and a screwdriver.

Jack up the car and support it with jack stands.

Locate the transmission cooler lines that run into the radiator, and inspect them for leaks.

Place a drain pan under the damaged lines. Remove the transmission cooler lines.

Install the new transmission cooler lines. Make sure the new lines are attached to the radiator, the transmission and any other hangers they may have been suspended from. Fill the transmission with the recommended fluid to the proper level.

Start the vehicle and check the transmission dipstick to make sure the fluid is at the proper level. Test-drive the vehicle to verify the repair.

How to Check Brake Fluid Level
First, check your brake fluid reservoir for the proper amount of brake fluid. Most reservoirs will have clear lines marking a minimum and maximum fluid level.

Fill the brake fluid reservoir with the manufacturer's recommended brake fluid. Do not spill any on the body of your vehicle. Brake fluid is like paint remover and will damage your car.

Once you have filled the tank, start your engine and step on the brake pedal a few times to check for proper pedal pressure.

Then verify the correct level of brake fluid in the reservoir.

Lastly, you may want to visually inspect the braking system for any signs of leaking. Consistently leaking brake fluid may pull air into the system and cause brake failure.

Kenny's Garage   Kenny Wallace

How to Perform a Brake Adjustment
You will need the following tools to perform this job: lug nut wrench, torque wrench, 3/8" drive ratchet, set of sockets, set of wrenches, flat head screwdriver, and a mallet.

First, let's determine if you need a brake adjustment. Pull your parking brake lever into its highest position possible. The ideal range is 4-7 clicks for rear drum brake types, and 5-8 clicks for rear disc brake types. If your parking brake is too tight or too loose, you need a brake adjustment.

To perform the brake adjustment, park your car on a level surface, and with a floor jack, lift the rear of the vehicle. Stabilize the car with jack stands before starting any work. Next, let's adjust the rear brake shoes. Go ahead and remove the rubber grommet from the little slot on the backing plate. Insert a screwdriver into the slot, and turn the star wheel to adjust the brake shoes out. You will want to adjust the star wheel until you feel a slight drag when spinning the wheel. Take your car out on the road to test how it feels.

You might also need to adjust your parking brake. So go ahead and remove the center console box.

At the rear of the handbrake lever, loosen the lock nut on the brake cable. Turn the adjusting nut until the parking brake travel is correct.

Finally, tighten the lock nut, and reinstall the console, and you are good to go.

How to Replace a Brake Booster
To replace the brake booster, you will need a new brake booster and brake fluid.
You will also need the following tools: torque wrench, 3/8' drive ratchet, set of sockets, set of wrenches, flat head screwdriver, and a mallet.

It is very easy to confirm a defective brake booster. With the engine off, step on the brake pedal several times to relieve the brake booster of vacuum. Then, press the brake pedal down, and start the engine. Normally, the brake pedal will sink slightly. If the brake pedal does not drop, then the brake booster has failed.

The first thing to do is locate the brake booster within the engine compartment. You need to remove the vacuum hose from the brake booster.

You also need to remove the brake lines from the master cylinder, and then remove the master cylinder from the brake booster.

Next, disconnect the brake pedal from the push rod. Typically, this connection is made under the dash with a simple c-clip or pin.

Loosen the nuts that hold the brake booster to the firewall, usually on the interior of the firewall under the dash, and have someone support the booster from inside the engine compartment. Then remove the old brake booster.

Install the new brake booster. Mount the booster back onto the firewall by tightening the bolts on the interior. Reconnect the push rod to the pedal. Reconnect the master cylinder back to the brake booster. And reconnect the brake lines.

Finally, bleed the brakes at the master cylinder. Before attempting to drive on the road, make sure you have a solid feeling brake pedal. If it feels spongy, bleed the entire system.

How to Replace the Brake Calipers
You will need a new set of brake calipers for this replacement job. To inspect and replace the brake calipers, you will also need a lug nut wrench, torque wrench, 3/8" drive ratchet, set of sockets, flat head screwdriver and a mallet.
Go ahead and remove the lug nuts on the front wheel and pull the wheel off the axle. Now you can visually inspect

the brake caliper for any signs of binding. Look for dirt build-up on the caliper slides or a lack of lubricant. You may also see uneven brake wear. If you notice the brake caliper binding, it will need to be replaced.

The first thing to do is remove the brake caliper mounting or sliding bolts. Then, remove the brake caliper. Support the caliper up and away from the working area with a bungee cord or a piece of wire. Do not allow the caliper to hang from the brake hose.

Clean the sliding bolts and lubricate them.

Install the new caliper over the brake pads and rotor. Attach the caliper to the mounting bracket with the sliding bolts. Tighten the caliper sliding bolts.

Remove the old caliper from its hanging spot and disconnect the brake hose from the caliper. Attach the brake hose to the new caliper using new copper washers. Tighten the banjo bolt.

Fill the master cylinder with brake fluid and bleed the brake caliper.

Reinstall the wheel and torque the lug nuts. Verify that you have a solid brake pedal before you road test your new calipers.

Kenny's Garage   Kenny Wallace

How to Replace a Brake Drum

To replace the brake drums on your car, you will need a new set of brake drums.

You will also need the following tools: break cleaner, lug nut wrench, torque wrench, 3/8" drive ratchet, set of sockets, flat head screwdriver, and a mallet.

Park your vehicle on a solid level surface and chock the front wheels. Loosen the rear wheel lug nuts, but do not remove.

Lift up the rear of the vehicle and support it with jack stands. Remove the rear wheel lug nuts. Remove the rear wheels and set them aside.

Remove the brake drum by pulling it outward. Make sure the parking brake is released. If the drum is stuck, use a mallet to break it loose.

Carefully inspect the drum for any discoloration, cracking, scoring, or grooving. If the drum is damaged, there is a good chance the brake shoes are worn. Replacing the brake shoes with the drum is usually recommended.

Spray the inside of the new drum with brake cleaner and wipe it off. Install the new drum. You can then put the wheel back onto the car, and torque the lug nuts to the manufacturer's specifications.

Next, remove the rubber grommet from the backing plate. Insert a screwdriver into the slot, and turn the star wheel to adjust the brake shoes out. Turn the star wheel adjuster until you feel a slight drag while spinning the wheel. Finally, road test the vehicle to ensure it is performing properly.

How to Flush Brake Fluid
You will need fresh brake fluid for this task.
You will also need the following tools: a set of flare nut wrenches, can of brake cleaner, shop rag, turkey baster or battery filler, clear plastic tube, and a container.

First, locate the brake reservoir within the engine compartment. Inspect the brake fluid for possible contamination. If it is dark, you will need to evacuate the fluid from the reservoir. I like to use a turkey baster. It's an easy way to pull fluid from the chamber.

Once you have removed the fluid, refill the reservoir with new brake fluid. Check your car manual for specific types of fluid.

Next, you need to bleed the brake system. Park your car on a flat surface, and remove the passenger side rear wheel. Locate the brake bleeder valve on your passenger side rear brake.

Install a piece of clear plastic tubing over the brake bleeder screw and place the other end into a container that is ½ full of brake fluid.

Place a 1"x4" block of wood under the brake pedal to prevent the pedal from moving too far. Now, have an assistant slowly depress and hold the brake pedal down. Crack the bleeder valve open. You will notice old fluid and air bubbles traveling down the clear tubing and into the container. Tighten the bleeder valve.

Repeat this process until clean fluid comes out of the bleeder valve and there are no more bubbles. Check and refill the master cylinder. Do not allow the master cylinder to drain completely.

Now, repeat the same steps for the left rear wheel, then the right front wheel, and finally the left front wheel. Then place the wheels back on the car, and verify that you have a solid brake pedal before road testing the vehicle.

How to Perform a Front Disc Brake Job
To perform a front disc brake job, you will need new brake rotors and brake pads. To complete this job, you will need the following tools: lug nut wrench, torque wrench, a set of sockets and ratchet, a set of wrenches, a flat head

screwdriver and a mallet.

Inspect your vehicle's brake pad thickness and inspect the brake rotors for grooves and discoloration. If the pads are worn and the rotors are damaged, then you will need to perform a front disc brake job.

Remove the brake caliper mounting bolts. Slide the brake caliper off of the brake rotor. Support the brake caliper up and away from the working area with a bungee cord or wire. Do not allow the caliper to hang from the brake hose. Do not disconnect the brake hose.

Remove the brake pads from the brake caliper. Remove the old rotor from the hub. Install a new brake rotor on the hub. Next, compress the caliper piston using a C-clamp. Install the new brake pads in the brake caliper. And reinstall the brake caliper.

Torque the brake caliper mounting bolts to the manufacturer's specifications. Repeat for the other side. Re-install the wheels and torque the lug nuts to the manufacturer's specifications.
Refill the brake fluid in the brake master cylinder and then reinstall the cap.

Then road test the vehicle to break in the new pads and rotors.

Kenny's Garage   Kenny Wallace

How to Replace a Master Cylinder

To replace the master cylinder, you will need a new brake master cylinder and brake fluid.

Additionally, you will need: lug nut wrench or tire iron, torque wrench, set of sockets and ratchet, set of wrenches, flat head screwdriver, mallet, turkey baster, bench bleeder kit and a clear vinyl tube with container.

Open your hood and locate the master cylinder mounted to the firewall on the driver's side. Inspect the brake fluid level.

If the fluid level is ok, then step on your brake pedal. Does it drop all the way to the floor? If so, you will know you have a faulty brake master cylinder.

Using a turkey baster or battery filler, remove all of the brake fluid from the master cylinder. (If you spill any fluid, quickly wash it off with water. It will take the paint off your car if not removed immediately).

Remove the brake lines from the master cylinder with a set of flare nut wrenches. Then disconnect any electrical connectors.

Unbolt the brake master cylinder from the brake booster. Add brake fluid and bleed the new master cylinder. Install the new master cylinder to the brake booster. Make sure you line up the brake booster's rod with the master cylinder's piston.

Reinstall the brake lines. And then fill the master cylinder reservoir with brake fluid.

Bleed the brakes at the master cylinder and verify that you have a solid brake pedal. If the pedal is sponge, bleed the entire system.

How to Replace Brake Pads
To replace your brake pads, you will need new brake pads, brake cleaner and anti-squeal lubricant.
You will also need the following tools: lug nut wrench or tire iron, torque wrench, flat head screwdriver, set of sockets with ratchet, C-clamp, jack stands and floor jack.

Inspect the thickness of the brake pads. If the pads are less than 1/8 inch thick, you will need to replace them.
First, remove the brake caliper mounting bolts and slide the brake caliper off the brake rotor. Support the brake caliper up and away from the working area with a bungee cord or wire. Do not allow the caliper to hang from the brake hose.

Do not disconnect the brake line.

Remove the brake pads from the brake caliper. Compress the caliper piston using a C-clamp.

Install the new brake pads in the brake caliper.

Reinstall the brake caliper and torque the mounting bolts to the manufacturer's specifications.

Finally, put the wheels back on, and make sure your brake fluid level is appropriate. Then road test your vehicle to test and break in the new pads.

How to Replace a Brake Pedal Switch
You will need a new brake pedal switch.
You will also need the following tools: needle nose pliers, flashlight and a set of wrenches.

To test the brake pedal switch, turn your ignition switch to the on position. Step on the brake pedal and have an assistant inspect the rear brake lights.

If both of the brake lights are out, then you will want to inspect the brake pedal switch, on the brake pedal linkage. Be sure to check for 12 volts into and out of the switch. Turn the car OFF before attempting any electrical work. Now, disconnect the wiring harness from the brake pedal switch. This will allow you to disconnect the brake pedal switch from the brake pedal linkage.

Now you can remove the old brake pedal switch and replace it with the new one.

Reconnect the wiring harness to the switch, and then test your lights again to make sure you have fixed the problem.

How to Replace a Brake Disc (or Rotor)
For this task, you will need: new front brake rotors and brake cleaner.
You will also need the following tools: lug nut wrench or tire iron with breaker bar, a dial indicator, a micrometer, jack, jack stand and a torque wrench.

Measure the thickness of the brake disc with a micrometer and measure the disc run-out with a dial indicator. You will need to replace or resurface the disc if it does not meet the manufacturer's specifications.

Remove the brake caliper mounting bolts. Remove the brake caliper. Using a bungee cord, secure the caliper up and away from the rotor. Do not allow the caliper to hang from the brake hose.

Remove the brake pads. Remove the brake caliper-mounting bracket. Remove the brake rotor. Spray the new brake rotor with brake cleaner and wipe it off. Install the

Kenny's Garage   Kenny Wallace

new brake rotor.

Re-install the brake caliper mounting bracket and disc pads. Torque the mounting bolts to the manufacturer's specifications. Re-install the brake caliper. Torque the caliper bolts to the manufacturer's specifications.
Put the wheel back on, and apply your brakes several times to test the repair.

How to Perform a Brake Safety Inspection
For this task you will need the following tools: floor jack, jack stands, lug nut wrench or tire iron, rubber mallet, flashlight, a torque wrench and socket.

Park your vehicle on a solid level surface. Open the hood and check the brake fluid in the master cylinder. The color should be clear and the fluid level within specifications. If the color is dark, the fluid should be changed. If the level is low, there may be a leak.

Lift up the vehicle and support it with jack stands. Remove the wheels. Remove the rear brake drums if necessary. Inspect the brake pads and shoes for even wear and proper thickness. They should have at least 25% of the lining left. Inspect the brake calipers for leaking or binding. Check the torque on the caliper mounting bolts with the manufacturer's specifications.

Next, inspect the brake rotors and drums for scoring, grooves, or discoloration from heat. Measure the rotor thickness and run out if you have a dial indicator and a micrometer.

Inspect the master cylinder, brake lines, and wheel cylinders for any fluid leaks. Make sure the brake hoses do not have any damage or cracks.

Re-install the brake drums (if necessary) and the wheels. Lower the vehicle to the ground and torque the wheel lug nuts to the manufacturer's specifications.

Verify that you have a solid brake pedal and test drive the vehicle. Your vehicle should stop straight without any noises or vibrations.

How to Replace the Brake Shoes
For this task, you will need the following part: new brake shoes.
You will also need the following tools: lug nut wrench or tire iron, torque wrench, set of sockets and ratchet, set of wrenches, flat head screwdriver, mallet, needle nose pliers and a brake drum diameter gauge.

The first thing you want to do is remove the brake drum. The parking brake will need to be fully released in order to do so. You will probably need to break the drum loose with a rubber mallet.

Inspect the brake shoes carefully. If the brake shoes are less than 1/8 inch thick, they will need replacing.

To replace the brake shoes, first remove the primary and secondary brake shoe return springs from the anchor pin and brake shoes. The primary spring is connected to the front brake shoe; the secondary spring is connected to the rear brake shoe.

Go ahead and remove the adjuster cable spring assembly. Remove the star adjusting screw and thread the adjuster all the way in.

Remove the front brake shoe retainer. Remove the front brake shoe and the parking brake link. Remove the parking brake lever from the rear brake shoe. Then remove the rear brake shoe retainer and remove the rear brake shoe.

Apply white lithium grease to the backing plate contact points. Install the new brake shoes in reverse order of removal, and be very careful to keep them clean. Inspect the drum and replace if necessary. Install the brake drum and adjust the brake shoes.

Finally put the wheels back on, and test-drive the vehicle to check your repair work.

Kenny's Garage　　　　　　　　　　　Kenny Wallace

How to Bleed Brakes with a Tool and with a Helper
For this task, you will need the following parts: brake fluid. You will also need the following tools: set of flare nut wrenches, 1/4" clear vinyl tubing and a clear container.

The first thing you should do is road test the vehicle. While braking, if the brake pedal feels soft or sinks to the floor, then you will know it is necessary to bleed the brakes. Lift rear of car. Jack stands… etc.

The first step in bleeding the brakes is to remove all of the old brake fluid from the master cylinder with a turkey baster. Then refill the master cylinder with new, clean brake fluid.

Place a 1"x4" block of wood under the brake pedal to prevent the pedal from moving. Then, locate the bleeder valve on the right rear wheel.

Install a piece of clear plastic tubing over the brake bleeder valve and insert the other end into a clear container, filled with 2-3 inches of clean brake fluid. Then have your assistant slowly depress and hold the brake pedal down.

Crack the bleeder valve open. Old fluid and air bubbles will travel down the clear tubing and into the container. Tighten the bleeder valve. Repeat this process until clean fluid comes out of the bleeder valve, refilling the master cylinder

Kenny's Garage Kenny Wallace

if necessary, as you do not want it to go empty.

Repeat for all of the wheels, and make sure your brake pedal is solid before road testing your car.

How to Check Power Steering Fluid Level
For this task, you will need the following part: power steering fluid.
You will also need the following tool: flashlight.

Go ahead and open the hood and locate the power steering fluid reservoir, usually toward the front of the car.
Then open the reservoir cap and inspect the condition of the power steering fluid. If the fluid is dark, it may be contaminated and needs to be replaced.

Add power steering fluid to the appropriate level between the minimum and maximum indicator levels.
Finally, road test the vehicle to make sure you can turn the steering wheel properly.

How to Replace a Power Steering Pump
In order to replace a power steering pump, you will need a new power steering pump and power steering fluid.
You will also need a drive ratchet, a set of sockets, a set of flare nut wrenches, a flat-head screwdriver and a fluid evacuator.

Kenny's Garage   Kenny Wallace

Open the hood and locate the vehicle's power steering pump and check the fluid level. Start the vehicle and have someone turn the steering wheel while you listen for a growling noise.

Turn the engine off and wait until its cold before reopening the hood and locating the power steering drive belt. Remove the belt. Place a drain pan under the power steering pump, and disconnect the power steering lines.

Remove the power steering pump mounting bolts. Take the pump off of the mounting bracket and install a new power steering pump on the mounting bracket. This may require transferring the old pulley to the new power steering pump with a puller tool.

Reconnect the lines to the power steering pump and reinstall the drive belt. Adjust the belt tension and torque bolts to fit the manufacturer's specifications.

Add power steering fluid to the reservoir and start the engine to circulate the fluid. Stop the engine before refilling the reservoir.

Restart the engine and turn the steering wheel from left to right. Take the vehicle for a road test to verify that the steering pump repair was successful.

Kenny's Garage   Kenny Wallace

How to Replace the Power Steering Rack

For this task, you will need the following parts: power steering rack, power steering fluid and cotter pins. You will also need the following tools: lug nut wrench or tire iron with breaker bar, torque wrench, 3/8" drive ratchet, set of sockets, set of flare nut wrenches, flat head screwdriver and a fluid evacuator.

Lift front of car. Use jack stands. Remove front wheel. Inspect the power steering system for any leaks. Also, turn on the car, and listen for any noises from the power steering system while turning the wheel. If you discover any leaks, you need to replace the power steering rack.

First, open the hood and locate the power steering reservoir. Using a turkey baster, remove all of the fluid from the chamber.

Lift front of car. Use jack stands. Remove front wheel. Remove the outer tie rod end cotter pins. You will need to replace the cotter pins during reassembly with new ones. Loosen the outer tie rod end nuts a few turns, but do not remove them yet.

Using the puller tool, separate the outer tie rod ends from the steering knuckles. Then remove the castle nuts completely. Be sure to secure the steering wheel straight ahead with a bungee.

Then remove the power steering lines from the power steering rack and remove the power steering rack.

Install the new power steering rack in the reverse order. Top off the power steering fluid in the reservoir and start the car for a minute and then shut it off.

Top off the power steering fluid again.

Then, start the car, and try turning the steering wheel. It should be perfect!

How to Replace the Coil Springs
For this task, you will need the following parts: new coil springs and coil spring mounts.
You will also need the following tools: wrenches, sockets and ratchets and a coil spring compressor.

Lift rear of vehicle. Use jack stands….

Ok, now take a look under the vehicle and inspect the coil springs to see if they are damaged. They could be cracked or broken, and if so, will need replacing immediately.

To access the coil springs, remove any lines or suspension components that are in the way. Accessing the front coil springs will require more steps such as removing the tires, shocks, and tie rod ends.

Please note that compressed coil springs store a tremendous amount of energy. This energy must be controlled and released slowly. Therefore, connect the coil spring compressor to the spring. Follow the instructions on your specific tool to do this.

Now you can lower the floor jack to remove the spring from its seats.

Remove the coil spring compressor tool from the old spring. And attach the tool to the new coil spring to compress it.

Insert the new coil spring into position.

Reattach any suspension components that were removed. Once you have all of the components reassembled you may then remove the coil compressor tool.

Remove the vehicle from the jack stands and drive to test the new springs.

How to Replace a Ball Joint
You will need a new ball joint for this repair.

Kenny's Garage   Kenny Wallace

You will also need a lug nut wrench or tire iron, a torque wrench, a set of sockets and ratchet, a set of wrenches, a hammer, a long pry bar, and a ball joint removal tool.

Support the lower control arm with a floor jack close to the ball joint. Remove the cotter pin from the ball joint retaining nut. Loosen the nut by turning it a few times.

Next, separate the ball joint from the knuckle by using a ball joint separator. Remove the nut, and secure the knuckle out of the way. Using a ball joint installation and removal tool, press the ball joint out of the lower control arm. Press the new ball joint into the control arm using the installation and removal tool. Reinstall the steering knuckle back onto the control arm/ball joint assembly.

Torque the castle nut to the manufacturer's specifications. Install a new cotter pin.

Re-install the wheels. Torque the lug nuts to the manufacturer's specifications. After replacing suspension components, always have the alignment checked at a certified repair shop.

How to Replace the Air Intake Boot
For this task, you will need the following part: air intake boot.

Kenny's Garage   Kenny Wallace

You will also need the following tools: flashlight set of sockets and ratchet, nut drivers and a screwdriver.

First, open the hood, and locate the air intake boot. Inspect the boot carefully for any cracks, holes, or loose components. If there is a crack or any damage, it will need replacing.

Loosen the clamps and remove the air intake boot. Install the new air intake boot with the original clamps. If there are any vacuum lines that are cracking from old age, it is a good idea to replace those as well.

Start the car, and listen for any hissing sounds.

How to Replace a Serpentine Belt
For this task, you will need the following parts: replacement serpentine belt; possibly a replacement belt tensioner and idler pulley.
You will also need the following tools: flashlight, 3/8" drive ratchet, set of sockets, set of wrenches, serpentine belt removal tool.

Open the vehicle's hood and take the key out of the ignition. Locate the vehicle's serpentine belt. Always make sure the shocks on your hood can fully support the weight so that it does not close on you while working. If necessary, use a hood prop tool to support the hood. Make sure the engine is off and cold before inspecting the serpentine belt to prevent any burns or injuries.

Inspect the ribs on a serpentine type belt. Look to see if there are any cracks or chunks missing. Look for any oil that was spilled on the belt or if the belt is wet.

Check the belt tension by pushing down in the middle of a section of the belt. A belt will become glazed when belt tension is too loose.

Locate the serpentine belt tensioner. It is a good idea to draw a diagram on how the serpentine belt is routed. Not all vehicles have an image of how the belt is routed under the hood.

Move the tensioner to create slack in the belt and remove the old serpentine belt.

Install the new serpentine belt making sure the belt is routed the same way as before. When installing the serpentine belt, make sure the serpentine belt is fully seated in the groove of the pulleys.

Check the belt tension by pushing down in the middle section of the belt. If the belt tension is too loose, the belt tensioner will need to be replaced.

Start the engine and allow the car to run for a few minutes to ensure proper belt installation. Do not touch the belt while the engine is running.

How to Replace a V-Belt
For this task, you will need the following part: new V-belt. You will also need the following tools: 3/8" drive ratchet, a set of sockets, a set of wrenches, and small pry bar or screwdriver.

Open the hood and listen for the V-belt that is making noise. Then shut off the car and inspect the belt carefully for damage. If the belt is damaged, it will need to be replaced.

Remove the old belt. Install the new belt, routing it the same way as before. Most vehicles will have a belt routing diagram under the hood. Be sure to follow this example if one is provided.

Turn the car on to make sure you do not hear the chirping or squealing noise.

How to Replace an Ignition Coil
For this task, you will need: a replacement ignition coil, and possibly replacement spark plugs, spark plug wires, and a cap and rotor.

Kenny's Garage   Kenny Wallace

You will also need: a test light, a spark tester, wrenches, a set of sockets and a ratchet.

Open the hood and locate the vehicle's ignition coil. Remove the coil wire to the distributor cap. Then, connect the spark tester to the coil wire. Crank the engine and check for a spark. If there is no spark, confirm that the coil wire is good and then test the ignition coil.

Follow the wiring diagram to determine if the coil is power, or groundside controlled. If ground-controlled, connect the test light clip to the power side of the battery and touch the test light to the negative side of the coil. Then, crank the engine and look for the test light bulb to flash.

If the ignition is power-side controlled, reverse the test light connections.

Disconnect the negative battery terminal and electrical connections to the coil, and remove the coil wire to cap. Remove the ignition coil from the vehicle and install the new ignition coil.

Start up the vehicle again and perform a road test to see if the ignition coil is working properly.

Kenny's Garage Kenny Wallace

How to Replace an Engine Freeze Plug

For this task, you will need the following parts: freeze plugs and coolant.

You will also need the following tools: radiator pressure tester, flashlight, hammer, pliers, punch and a large socket.

Locate the engine block freeze plugs on your car, usually within the engine compartment on the sides of the engine block.

Use a cooling pressure tester to pressurize the system. If you notice any leaks from the freeze plug, you will need to replace it.

Place a drain pan under the radiator. Open the drain valve or remove the lower radiator hose to drain the engine coolant.

Strike the inside edge of the leaking freeze plug with a hammer and punch. Remove the leaking freeze plug. Clean the engine block hole with emery cloth. Using a large socket, hammer in the new freeze plug evenly.

Now, close the drain valve or reconnect the lower radiator hose and fill the radiator with coolant. Once again, pressurize the system to check for any leaks.

Kenny's Garage   Kenny Wallace

How to Clean Your Fuel System
For this task, you will need fuel and fuel system cleaner. You may also need a fuel filter, fuel lines or a fuel tank if any of these need replacing.

Drive the vehicle to see how it performs, which is a good indicator of the fuel system's condition. Keep in mind that the mileage and condition of the engine can also contribute to its performance.

If you have a clear fuel filter, check the color of the fuel. It should not be dark. Consider smelling the fuel to see if it has gone bad or not. Bad fuel will smell like varnish.

Check the fuel tank for cracks, and make sure the fuel lines are in good shape. If these are not in optimum condition, they will need to be replaced.

Add a fuel system additive to the fuel tank, and top off the fuel level with new gas according to the directions on the additive.

Test-drive the vehicle to see if there is an improvement in its performance.

How to Replace a Catalytic Converter
For this task, you will need the following part: catalytic converter.

Kenny's Garage   Kenny Wallace

You will also need the following tools: rubber mallet, set of sockets and ratchet, reciprocating saw and a set of wrenches.

Park your vehicle on a solid level surface. Lift the vehicle and support it with jack stands.

Loosen the clamps that hold the catalytic converter to the exhaust pipes. If your catalytic converter is welded on, you will need to cut it off with a reciprocating saw.

If necessary, remove the exhaust pipe from the manifold. Clean all of the mounting surfaces and remove burrs on the metal pipes to allow the new converter to slide on easier. Install the new converter. The converter needs to be placed in the correct direction, so check for the arrow on the converter that points in the direction of the exhaust flow. Install the exhaust clamps and tighten the nuts securely. You may find it necessary to re-install the exhaust pipe to the manifold.

Start the vehicle and check for exhaust leaks.

How to Replace a Wiper Blade
For this task, you will need the following part: wiper blade. You will also need the following tool: screwdriver.

First, locate the windshield wipers.

Inspect the wiper blades for cracking, torn rubber, wear or stiffness.

Then, pull the spring loaded wiper arm up.

Remove the blade assembly from the wiper arm. Most wiper blades have a plastic tab that when depressed and pushed down, will make the wiper arm assembly slide out. Next, install the new wiper blade assembly. It will either snap into place on the arm, or clip onto the blade ends.

Bend the tabs once the new blade is installed.

Remember to test the new windshield wiper blade for proper operation.

How to Replace a Wiper Motor
For this task, you will need the following parts: replacement wiper motor.
You will also need the following tools: test light, set of sockets, ratchet, pocket screwdriver.

First, locate the wiper motor in the engine compartment on the firewall. For the rear wiper motor, you may need to remove the rear hatch interior trim panel to gain access to the unit.

Kenny's Garage   Kenny Wallace

Check the wiper motor fuse located in the main fuse box. The owner's manual will give a diagram of the fuses and location as well.

Then, gain access to the wiper motor assembly.

Turn the ignition switch on. Turn the windshield wiper switch to the on position.

Next, with the test light, check for power and ground at the motor. To check for power, clip the test light to the negative terminal of the battery and touch the tip of the test light to the positive side of the wiper motor. To check for ground, clip the test light to the positive terminal of the battery and touch the tip of the test light to the negative side of the wiper motor.

Turn the ignition switch off. Disconnect the negative battery cable.

Disconnect the wiper arm assembly and wiring harness from the motor.

Remove the wiper motor mounting bolts and remove the motor.
Install the new wiper motor.

Install the mounting bolts and torque to the manufacturer's specifications.

Connect the electrical harness.

Next, connect the wiper arm assembly to the motor.

Finally, connect the negative battery cable.

Remember to test the wiper motor operation at all speeds and verify the repair.

How to Replace a Wiper Switch
For this task, you will need the following part: replacement wiper switch.
You will also need the following tools: test light, ratchet, set of sockets, pocket screwdriver, digital multimeter.

First, turn the key to the on position to provide power to all interior accessories.

Then, locate the wiper switch mounted to the steering column.

Turn the wiper switch to the on position.

Next, inspect the wipers for proper operation while selecting different speeds. Using a test light, you can check the wiper switch for power and ground. You will need a factory wiring diagram in order to identify the difference between which wires are power and ground.

Then, turn the key to the off position. Disconnect the negative battery cable.

Disconnect the wiring harness from the switch.

Remove the old switch and replace it with a new switch.

Connect the wiring harness to the new switch.

Finally, connect the negative battery cable.

Remember to test the wiper switch for proper operation to verify the repair.

Some Easy Odds and Ends

How to Adjust a Hood Release Latch

In order to adjust your hood latch, you will need a 3/8" drive ratchet, a set of sockets, and a set of open end wrenches.

First, loosen the bolts on the hood latch just enough to be able to move the latch a little. Move the latch to either side to align it with the opening inside the hood inner panel. Loosen the lock nuts on the two hood stops and lower the stops.

Move the hood latch up or down to obtain a flush fit between the top of the hood and the fenders when an upward pressure is applied to the front of the hood.

Next, tighten the hood latch mounting bolts. Then raise the two hood stops to eliminate any looseness at the front of the hood when it is closed, and tighten the lock nuts.

Finally, you should open and close the hood several times to ensure you have done the job properly.

How to Replace a Hood Emblem

For this task, you will need a replacement emblem.

You will also need a flat head screwdriver, a shop rag, cleaner and glue.

Determine how the damaged emblem is mounted by inspecting it thoroughly. Sometimes the emblem is screwed in from underneath, so opening the hood might be necessary.

Remove the damaged emblem. If an adhesive attached it, clean the area thoroughly before continuing.
Install the new emblem by sticker adhesive, automotive glue, screws or tabs.

If the new emblem was attached by glue or adhesive, allow it to sit and dry for at least two hours before driving.

How to Replace a Window Belt Strip
In order to replace the window belt strips, you will need new belt strips.
You will also need needle nose pliers, and a pocket screwdriver.

Locate the window belt strips around your windows. Visually inspect the belt strips for cracking or damage. If there is damage to the belt strip, you will want to replace it. First, lower the window to its lowest position. Use a small pocket screwdriver to carefully pry out the belt strip from the door panel.

Once you have pried the strip out, use a pair of needle nose pliers to carefully pull the belt strip out of position and away from the clips. Be very careful not to scratch the paint of the interior door panels.

Next, snap the new belt strip into place using the existing clips. If a clip breaks, you will need to replace it.
Finally, once the strip is installed, go ahead and roll the window all the way up to make sure it is properly sealed and fitted.

How to Troubleshoot a Check Engine Light
For this task, you will need an OBD Scanner.
First, locate the check engine light and monitor its status. You need to run the vehicle in order to verify that it stays on consistently.

Step two; connect the scanner to the OBD II output. In 1995, OBD II was introduced, and all connectors were standardized by 1996. Retrieve the diagnostic trouble code with the OBD II Scanner.

You may receive one code, or you may receive five. Troubleshoot all possible symptoms that relate to the diagnostic trouble code or codes.

Kenny's Garage   Kenny Wallace

Once you diagnose the problem that causes your check engine light to come on, you must replace whatever the faulty component is. When you replace the faulty component, use the OBD II Scanner to erase the trouble code.

Now, start the car and monitor the check engine light again. If your light is off, it means you have fixed the problem successfully. If the light is on, it means you still have a hard code present, and need to continue troubleshooting the problem.

Closing Thoughts

Long term, what can people do to make sure they continue to enjoy their car?

Take care of the car. Don't just take it to the car wash every Saturday. The old theory of, "My car runs better when it's clean," doesn't work. Mechanical maintenance is so important, not only for resale value but for performance. Pop the hood when you're pumping gas and check your fluids. Have the oil changed every 3,000 miles unless you are running on synthetic. Things like this will keep your car healthy. Also, run the right gas in your car. Keep it as healthy as you possibly can.

And don't be afraid to use it! Especially if you have a sports car, don't let it sit in your driveway so that the fluid systems get clogged up. Drive it around at least once a week. Equate the car to your body. You want it running well and you don't want it to get all clogged up.

Take care of your ride and your ride will take care of you! Keep it clean inside and out. Your car is your home on wheels.

Kenny Wallace Bio

Kenny Wallace won the first race he ever entered in 1982. Kenny's win at the Springfield Fairgrounds, mile long dirt track in Springfield, Illinois would be the first of many in his racing career. After winning that first race, Kenny decided that his place in racing was in the driver's seat. In 1986, Kenny joined the ASA ranks winning Rookie of the Year honors.

Kenny is the youngest of the three Wallace boys, and racing was a household reality before any of the boys could drive a car. Track promoter Bob Miller at the Lake Hill Speedway in Valley Park, Missouri noticed Kenny's boisterous behaviour and started calling him "Herman" after a mischievous cartoon character named Herman the German. The nickname has stuck through Kenny's rise through the racing ranks.

He is the winner of the first Tony Stewart "Prelude to the Dream" at Eldora Speedway in 2005.

Kenny is the only driver to have won the Nationwide Series Most Popular Driver Award three times, Kenny ranks number one with the most starts in NASCAR Nationwide series history with nine wins in this series.

Kenny's most well-known finish came when he pushed the late great Dale Earnhardt to his final Cup victory at Talladega in 2000 in a thrilling last lap shootout. Kenny ranks 13th out of 4000 drivers in the overall history of NASCAR starts with 900!

Kenny is the co-host on NASCAR Raceday, NASCAR Victory Lane, and NASCAR Coverage on FOX Sports 1 each week. With Kenny's competitive battles on the racetrack and popularity on television, he has become one of the most sought after drivers in NASCAR racing for sponsor endorsements and speaking engagements.

Kenny Wallace is a driver that is well respected by owners, drivers and sponsors throughout the garage area and racing community.

On almost any weekend, you can find Kenny getting back to the roots of short track racing in his #36 dirt modified.

Kenny is thrilled to release this book "Kenny's Garage" and is excited to assist car owners with their cars.

Credits

Foreword by: Kenny Schrader
Edited by: Sharon Long
Graphic Designer: Karen Davis
Front cover photo credit: Mike Campbell Photos
Back cover photo credit: Brittney Rosberg